Tales From the
Country Matchmaker

Patricia Warren

Tales From the
Country Matchmaker

HODDER

First published in Great Britain in 2003 by Farming Books and Videos
First published by Hodder & Stoughton in 2005
This paperback edition published by Hodder & Stoughton in 2006
A division of Hodder Headline

A Hodder paperback

1

A CIP catalogue record for this title is available from the British Library

0 340 89493 8

Illustration by Helen Chapman

Typeset in Sabon by Hewer Text UK Ltd, Edinburgh
Printed and bound by Clays Ltd, St Ives plc

Hodder Headline's policy is to use papers that are natural, renewable
and recyclable products and made from wood grown in sustainable forests.
The logging and manufacturing processes are expected to conform to
the environmental regulations of the country of origin.

Hodder and Stoughton Ltd
A division of Hodder Headline
338 Euston Road
London NW1 3BH

Acknowledgements

I wish to thank all those friends who continually badgered me to write this book, and in particular, Jill Tait and Rosina Newton for their constructive criticism and encouragement; my children who were so patient with me throughout those months and most of all, my husband, John, for his constant help, suggestions and continual support. He says he's a saint for putting up with me – he probably is.

Above all, without the hundreds of Bureau clients who have let me be part of their lives, this book would never have been written. They have given me their friendship and allowed me to record their sad, exciting, lonely and happy moments. I sincerely thank them all.

Contents

1. Make Hay While the Sun Shines   1

2. Little Dolly Daydream   22

3. The Farmer Wants a Wife   52

4. The Perfect Match   78

5. Go Forth and Multiply   89

6. What's for You Won't Go by You   105

7. The North Wind Doth Blow . . .   125

8. A Nice Guy   143

9. Quaint Old English Customs   153

10. Hearts and Flowers and Sleepless Nights   162

11. The Lonely Furrow   170

12. A Tall Order   188

13. Come Live with Me and Be My Love . . .   200

14. It Takes All Sorts   211

15. Gather Ye Rosebuds   237

I

Make Hay While the Sun Shines

One peaceful summer morning I was crossing the farmyard in a leisurely fashion on my way to my office. It was very early and as I gazed across the fields the mist was still hanging in the valley, with the promise of a hot sunny day ahead. Suddenly the phone started ringing. I quickened my step and hastened to pick up the receiver, preparing myself for the usual polite, 'Good morning. Patricia Warren speaking, the Farmers and Country Bureau.' But the caller didn't give me a chance – he just waded straight in.

'George 'ere. That lass you fixed me up wi', she's no bloody good. Too tight wi' 'er money.'

I wasn't too fazed, but this was very plain speaking indeed for six o'clock in the morning. It was obvious that he was a Yorkshireman, and after a few seconds my brain clicked into gear and I remembered who he was.

'Oh, it's you, George. Well, I'm sorry to hear things aren't working out with you and Joan. You've been going out for quite a while, haven't you? I take it that you won't want to see her again. But you know, you should really tell her that yourself if you feel you can.'

'Now, Mrs Warren,' he continued – and I could tell I

was in for some Yorkshire reasoning here, 'I didna say that I want to stop seein' 'er – not just yet like, an' I'll tell thee for why. What it is, she's knittin' me a jumper – 'er an' me mother between 'em. She's doin' the body and me mother's knittin' the sleeves. So I canna finish wi' 'er till it's all joined up, else it'll be a waste o' good wool. But I dunna want 'er for a wife, cus 'er 's too tight wi 'er money – an' dunna thee worry, I shall tell her so when t'jumper's finished.'

My mouth dropped open at his words. I couldn't believe the irony of George telling me he was going to keep on with Joan so as not waste any wool in the same breath as he criticised her for being tight. I had to bring the conversation to an end quickly and put the phone down before I burst out laughing. I tend to think I've come across every kind of man that God has made and every form of human courtship in the universe, from the suave and sophisticated to blunderings beyond belief, but this was truly the limit.

In my business a sense of humour is indispensable, and George had certainly given mine an early morning airing. Yet a lot of people treat introduction agencies with a sort of scornful humour, joking and sneering whenever the subject comes up. But often that kind of response just covers up an inability to take control of their own lives and do something positive about meeting someone special. The best approach is to aim for a balance, and treat joining a bureau quite light-heartedly – after all, life is fun and meeting others should be enjoyable and relaxed – but also treat it with the sincerity and significance that it deserves; because if it works, it can change the whole of someone's life.

I've been passionate about matchmaking all my life, right from my childhood when I used to pair up my dolls, and I'm pleased to say it has given me a huge amount of joy over the years. I feel that helping others to meet a life partner is a very worthwhile service to be providing. I regard it seriously and try to carry out my job to the very highest standards. In this respect I will not compromise, and I would never allow anyone to join the bureau who I thought for one moment would not give other members the respect they deserve. That's quite heavy stuff, you might say. Well, yes – but I am dabbling with people's lives, wishes, desires, hopes and expectations and I insist on doing my very best by a strict moral code – that has always been essential to me.

I couldn't settle down to work in the bureau that morning – George had made me laugh so much with his contradictions. My mind started to wonder about the incredible differences in human nature and how amazing it is that men and women ever get together – and stay together. But before I had had time to get too involved with my thoughts I had a phone call from Megan, a client who had been going out for nearly a year with David, a farmer from northwest Wales. Her voice was kind and soft, thoughtful, worldly and beautifully lilting with its deep Welsh accent. She began by saying she hadn't thought I would be in my office early on such a lovely summer day, then went on to tell me that she loved David very much and believed that he loved her also, but they

3

seemed to have run into difficulties. Could she talk this through with me and ask for a bit of advice?

'I love him dearly, but so often he just doesn't want to talk to me. I want him so much to tell me his feelings and be a bit romantic, but it's as if any show of emotion is taboo and he won't let it come to the surface.'

'I know what you mean, Megan,' I replied. 'Men are a breed apart – particularly those who, when they were growing up, never received any encouragement, from their parents to talk openly. It sounds as if David's very much like my husband.'

'Your husband!' Megan echoed. 'I wouldn't have thought you'd have chosen a man who couldn't show his feelings easily.'

'Well, I did. John's so bad at talking about his emotions that a few weeks ago, when he knew he really ought to try, it turned into a complete disaster.'

I told her about what had happened at my father's recent funeral. When a parent dies, it takes most people some time to come to terms with the idea that their mother or father is no longer in this world, and I too was constantly returning to thoughts about my father and feeling understandably emotional. I stood at the graveside, weeping and generally very sad, while John tried desperately to cheer me up. Looking down, he turned and toed with his shoe the fresh deep brown earth newly dug out around the grave. 'Never mind, love,' he murmured. 'He's in a good place here. Just look at the quality of the soil – it's really good stuff.'

I looked up at him, completely appalled and dumbfounded by his attempt to offer comfort. Then I saw the funny side of it – he had tried so hard to be reassuring, but his choice of words at this extremely emotional moment was just so inept.

Megan laughed with me, and agreed that men do seem to find it hard to talk about their feelings. Then she became serious again and described how she and David had drifted apart – all she wanted was to regain the closeness they had once had. At David's farm his son, who had recently joined his father, was constantly on the scene and this was rather disconcerting, although generally he was a lovely boy and she was very fond of him. I told Megan it sounded as if she and David needed to spend some time completely alone, and they should try to meet up somewhere one day a week, right away from the farm, somewhere central between her home and David's. She said the beauty spot of Bettws-y-Coed would be a good place, and when I suggested they book into a hotel there for the odd afternoon of indulgence, she said she thought I was being rather naughty. But, as I said to Megan, sometimes thinking outside the box can provide the right answer.

Rosie, my secretary at the time, was sitting in the office while I was taking the call and seemed to have picked up on what I was talking about. 'Oh yes, there are some lovely hotels in that area,' she said. 'I've visited most of them.'

'It wouldn't surprise me, the way you've been getting about recently,' I replied.

Rosie had started working for me about a year

previously, and at the time had been married for about twenty-five years to a local farmer. I like to employ staff who are involved with farming as they have a better understanding of my clients. She was in her fifties, well-built, with grey hair, and never wore make-up. After about six months in the job she parted from her husband and had since changed considerably, from being a quiet, unnoticed, nondescript woman to someone who was definitely enjoying life in all ways. Some mornings she would arrive in her car at great speed, saying she thought she'd never make it on time. Then she would explain she had just driven from the other side of the country to make the 9 a.m. start. Every time she would tell me she'd met up with a new friend (male) the previous evening and that time had just 'flown by', so she'd had to stay the night. With my naïve mind and unexciting married life-style I would marvel and laugh as she recounted her recent romantic exploits.

Then one day I started to piece together some of the remarks made to me by a number of the middle-aged gents on my register. They didn't want to have another introduction at the moment as they had been promised a date by a lady they had been speaking to recently. Rosie had been chatting up my clients and promising to meet up with them! When I questioned her about this I discovered that she had not gone ahead with any of these encounters, but it had got pretty close. Sadly, Rosie had to go as I could not countenance such conduct, but I missed the amusement her stories had afforded. This experience also taught me never to put anyone into a pre-set category just from outward appearances. The most dowdy, colourless-seeming character can have unimaginable talents hiding beneath the surface just waiting to get out.

In the twenty years that the bureau has been established I have of course employed a number of secretaries and got on well with them all. They usually stay for a long time, and then the seven-year itch afflicts them and pastures new beckon. My secretaries have been friends, babysitters, confidantes and companions, and very deep friendships have been cemented between us. None, however, would ever take on the task of doing the real 'dirty work' when it came to speaking plainly to difficult clients. Marjorie, a local farmer alongside her husband and son, worked part-time for me. Being the most mature of all my secretaries she did occasionally help me out by being very frank with some clients on the telephone, but when it came to the nitty-gritty in truly awful situations it was always left to me.

One farmer who came through the door smelt so badly that he outdid the muck cart which from time to time swept past on its way to the fields. Nevertheless I was pleasant and friendly to him, for I always try to put people at their ease. When I asked what sort of farming he did he said he reared pigs, and then I realised what the smell was. I took a deep breath to steady myself for some plain talking, and nearly passed out with the fumes. I asked if anything unusual had happened on the farm that day, thinking that maybe all the stock had got loose and he had not had time to shower or change his clothes, but he assured me everything was fine.

'Please forgive me for bringing this up,' I said, 'but would you go out with a lady in those clothes? They do smell a bit of pigs.'

Bristling with indignation, he told me he wouldn't stand for such insults and walked out of the office. When I'd had time to recover, I reflected that this reaction must have been a cover for his embarrassment. What a shame. But I don't know how else I could have approached the subject.

On another occasion I had to direct some plain speaking at Charles, a well-educated man in his early thirties. A graduate who had gone on to become an accountant and now worked for a large company in the Midlands, he had been brought up on a small farm but had been encouraged to 'go off and make something of your life'. He had told me previously that his parents had endured years of hard work with little reward and were determined that Charles would not end up in the same position: 'Get yourself a proper job and become an accountant!' Throughout his childhood he had followed their wishes, but in his twenties became totally frustrated because of the over-riding fact that he loved farming and hated accountancy. The lure of the countryside was so intense that he had actually bought himself a small farm which he worked at weekends. But the thing that was most noticeable about Charles was that he continually used bad language.

'The last bloody woman didn't work out,' he complained to me. 'Just like the others – this one didn't even bloody well phone back. It's a bugger really.'

I noticed from his file that he had received about five introductions, but none had gone any further than speaking on the telephone. Suddenly it dawned on me that he must have been using this terrible language in the course of phone conversations with women. How strange it seemed – it would be easier to accept this kind of language from a brusque old farmer than from a young professional. I knew I had to bring the problem out in the open.

'I don't know if you realise it, Charles, but you do swear quite a lot in your everyday conversation, even when you're on the phone.'

All went quiet at this chastisement, and I imagined his frown deepening at the other end of the phone line.

'I do a bit, don't I?' he replied in a subdued manner.

I told him that if he spoke to his potential partners as he spoke to me, it certainly wouldn't create a good impression. 'I want you to make a concerted effort not to let a single swearword escape from your lips when you speak to the next girl.'

'I'll certainly try, Pat,' he said, as meek and mild as a little lamb, obviously transported back to the days of a dragon of a schoolteacher laying down the rules and regulations.

'Well, that went rather well,' I said to myself as I got back to my paperwork.

More common than either of these problems, though, is the man who wants everything. I answered the phone one day to a broad country accent, slightly Welsh but with a hint of the lovely rural voice of Shropshire. He introduced himself as Ivor, and said he was a farmer who had never been married but was now looking for a wife.

'She's got to be a farmer's daughter working on her dad's farm. I don't want someone who goes out to work. Must never have been married. I don't really want her to have had boyfriends. Someone in her early thirties – I've thought about twenties, but I think that's a bit young for me.'

'Let's talk about you first,' I said.

Ivor told me that his father was very old and quite ill, and that the woman he was looking for must be prepared to look after him. He then added, 'Of course, I want children.' As I listened intently to his conversation little red warning lights started to appear in my mind.

'Tell me, Ivor,' I said, 'why does she have to be a farmer's daughter and working on her dad's farm?'

'In case I die,' he immediately replied.

'What do you mean?' I asked, imagining that this poor man knew he had a terminal illness.

'So that my son will have someone to look after the farm until he's old enough to take over.'

'You have a son?' I asked.

'Not yet,' he replied. 'But she will give me a son, and that is my plan afterwards in case I die.'

'But what if you didn't have a son? What if all the children you had were daughters? Or what if you and a future wife didn't even have children?'

'Well, she'd be no good for me if she couldn't have any children, would she?'

'But what if you were the infertility factor in all this?' I asked, just in the hope of shocking him. It then suddenly dawned on me that I'd better find out his age.

'Fifty-six,' came the reply.

'Gosh, Ivor!' I said. 'There aren't many ladies in their thirties on my files who would consent to be introduced to a man in his fifties, you know. The other fact is that any woman would want to be wanted for herself. She'd want to fall in love with you, and to expect the relationship itself to be the most special thing between you, not her ability to breed – and to breed only sons at that!'

The conversation that morning was by no means unique. Over the years hundreds of men around that age and older have approached the bureau with the sole aim of finding a means to produce a son and heir. The oldest was eighty-six! That summer seemed to be full of older men and the romance they wished to recapture in the autumn of their lives. And later on that summer I had to tread very carefully in a highly diplomatic and sensitive task connected with my father and the ladies in his life.

My parents had married at the onset of World War II in 1939, when they were eighteen and twenty respectively, having courted throughout their teenage years. They had a very happy marriage for over forty years and never deviated from their love and devotion to each other. Sadly, my mother died in her early sixties. Once by himself Dad decided to be positive, and went out and enjoyed every moment of the next ten years of his life. When he died, as sole executor of his Will I knew I had to read through the wording very precisely:

Any three framed prints, of her personal choice, by Sir William Russell Flint, to be given to Nanette Calander and also my statue of a nude female person which stands thirty inches tall. I also bequeath fifteen thousand pounds to the said Nanette Calander to be enjoyed by her without hindrance.

A print depicting a nude female lying on a bed to Joan Riley, and seven thousand pounds.

A statuette of a nude female and male persons entitled *The Union*, to Sarah Kelly.

A nude male and female bronze entitled *The Kiss*, to be given to Alice Johnson.

And so it went on and on, with exact instructions for the disposal of gifts to these ladies and a few others. I knew my visit to the family home in Worcestershire to carry out his wishes would be sad but laced with a little humour. I had to receive each of the ladies that my father called his 'girlfriends' at his house, and tell each about his bequests to them. The old devil had warned me beforehand and mischievously said, 'You'll have to sort it out for me after I've gone.'

For one naughty moment I did contemplate asking them all to attend a formal 'reading of the Will', but I quickly realised that this would be wrong of me – never mind how much I wanted to see the reaction of each lady as I dramatised the scene in my mind. So I was good, and first I saw Dad's most 'special' lady whom I know he loved very much.

Nanette and my father had been lovers for about nine

years and, although they spent most of their weekdays apart, they spent very sociable and exciting weekends together. I knew he met up with the other ladies for occasional evenings and days out, but none was in the same category as Nanette. Our meeting went rather well, really. Nanette and I spent most of the morning at Dad's house and then we had lunch together, after which she went off with her bequests safely placed in the back of her car.

In the afternoon each of the other ladies had been asked to arrive separately on the hour. I read out the relevant paragraph in the Will and then accompanied the lady in question to the appropriate part of the house and the scene of the erotic *objet d'art*. They all behaved rather as if they were my favourite grandmother, which felt strange when handing over such explicit images. And, as they weren't gift-wrapped, they were clearly visible to passers by as they were carried out of the house. I'd received instructions from Dad that to each item I was to attach a small card with the words: 'So you may contemplate what never was – but could have been.' The second lady read the card and cried a little, then placed her bequest in a large carrier bag. The third, the recipient of *The Union*, read the card, gave an almighty laugh and tucked the sculpture under her arm. The fourth, smiling at the words, placed *The Kiss* on the passenger seat next to her in her car.

'You wicked old man!' I repeated again as I talked to the walls around me, hoping my words might reverberate up to heaven – or quite possibly down to hell – to be heard by my old dad.

Knowing I was going to Worcestershire for a short while, I had accepted an invitation from two clients to visit them a little further south, in Gloucestershire. So the next day I journeyed down through Evesham, then on to Cheltenham and round the outskirts of Gloucester. I stopped and had lunch with a veterinary surgeon friend and his wife who have a farm in Gloucestershire, then descended slowly from a high escarpment into the valley below. I had a wonderful view of the county, only slightly dimmed by the heat haze on the beautiful summer afternoon. There were miles of fields in front of me dotted with the comings and goings of farming activity, and as the scene spread out I felt as if I could touch each individual field. It looked like a massive, brilliantly coloured patchwork quilt. Tractors and trailers were trundling to and fro. Men, some closer but others tiny in the distance, were busily jumping on and off machinery, walking around fields, directing other people. And all this was going on virtually everywhere. It reminded me of the pictures in my childhood Noddy books.

Carefully I wove my way along the narrow, high-hedged lanes – a bit of a lottery, really, as I couldn't see for more than a few yards ahead because of the frequent blind corners. As I dropped down into the lower land of the valley the pungent, warm, musky smell of hay hit me. It was so lovely and so overpowering that I stopped the car and took in huge breaths of that incredibly nostalgic smell. Tractors started trying to pass me but it was impossible, so I pulled up in a gateway and turned off the engine. The smell made me think about our family farm back home in Derbyshire, and I recalled our own days of haymaking.

We haven't made hay for over twenty years, and my husband John will claim that those who say 'What a pity' are never the people who actually worked every moment of the day and night to make it. 'Bloody hard work,' he would say. 'It's hot, sweaty and dirty, and if you've got to make up to twenty thousand bales you'll work harder than you've ever done in your life.'

As the farmer's wife, I remember being on a knife-edge in the early mornings. Will the weather be good enough for him to start mowing? You had to judge it just right so that you could mow and ted and row it all in succession to produce those much-wanted final bales. The stress would accumulate dramatically first thing in the morning as we all waited for John to make the decision – will he or won't he? We all wanted to get going, but he knew that making the wrong decision would result in the worst hay in the world. I would want him to get going for my own insignificant and selfish reason – so that my cakes and pies that I had made or bought for the men over the previous days wouldn't go stale.

'We're going!' I would hear him say – and then we all knew that for the next few days everything would be centred on getting the hay in. It was always a frenzied rush. We lived in fear of a breakdown, no matter how carefully the machinery had been prepared and serviced in the previous weeks. And it always happened. I, like all other farmers' wives, would be on call to get new parts instantly – take the curses, keep quiet no matter what he says to you! In my first year of marriage I was so upset because John started shouting at me when the machinery broke down, even though I'd done nothing to cause it, that I complained to my mother on the phone. 'He has to blame the injustices of a breakdown on someone,' she explained, 'and it can't be the men, so it has to be you. Your dad was just like that. Now keep quiet, keep out of the way and just pray that all will get going again soon.' The tension and stress at those difficult times seemed insurmountable.

It was always my job to fetch the men in the late afternoon and early evening to help with the carting – we would never leave a bale outside overnight in case it rained. Because we used to make such a lot we needed a lot of help in those summer evenings, and about twelve good men and true would come to help from the village of Youlgrave about two miles away. I would go out and help load, while John was always in the barn stacking. We all knew our jobs and the whole thing was usually done with great humour. It was important to keep the working men in a good mood, as their help at this time was so crucial. Cider and beer went around in abundance throughout the evening. It didn't really matter how much the men drank as long as it kept their thirst at bay and they kept working. After two or three hours' work I would go and take their tea out to the fields. There was a great deal of bantering and joking for the next half-hour, after which, suitably refreshed, they worked even harder.

Once it was dark and all the hay for that day was in and stacked, the men came to the house for meat and pickles and more drink. John just collapsed into bed. I washed up and thought about what food needed to be got for the next day.

With a good crop and the very last bale safely in, the feelings of relief were immense. The next day always we had a celebration supper at a local pub. All the men would come along, but this time well dressed and ready for a good time. We would provide a large meal and drink would flow in profusion. Goodbyes to the once-a-year casual men would be made, and when we got home I knew that John would have the best and most-deserved sleep of the year.

But now that was all in the past and these were only fond memories rekindled by the sight of these Gloucestershire haymakers. I roused myself from my daydreams and remembered what I was supposed to be doing that afternoon – I was visiting old clients, now married. I manoeuvred my car back on to the road and continued to negotiate the narrow rural lanes.

As I drove towards David and Katie that afternoon I wondered how this couple were getting on, as I always do when I am asked to come and visit. I remembered David as being in his early thirties, tallish and broad, with fair hair and a great smile. A farmer's son who worked as a blacksmith, he was as sincere and nice a person as you would ever wish to meet. When he first joined the bureau he had taken a hard knock with a previous romance and so was quite disillusioned and disheartened.

David had been realistic in his search for a partner. He

knew he had to meet more people in order to find that one special person, but meeting her through an introduction agency was not how he thought he was going to do it. As we talked, he told me how his original plan had been to find a nice rural pub which a country girl might use as her local. He decided that the Beacon Hotel at Haresfield, just three miles away, was a place where he might stand a chance, and he often went there, particularly on the nights when they had live music. But no matter how much he tried, he met no one. In the end he realised he needed another way of meeting people, and that was when he decided to join the bureau.

Katie was his first introduction, and he was the first person she met with the bureau. She was a lovely, single girl in her early thirties, a farmer's daughter who worked as a nursery nurse, with blonde hair and a warm and friendly face and nature. Katie had had boyfriends before and one in particular had been serious, but, just like David, she had been hurt.

But things had worked out well for these two deserving but emotionally damaged young people.

After arriving at their house, and with a refreshing long drink in my hand, I sat down and glanced around at this young couple's home. It was cottage-style, small and cosy, but with the advantages of being very new. Inside it was bright, cheerful and stylish, and all the walls were mellow yellow. Neat and obviously well cared for, it perfectly reflected their personalities.

David had been astounded when he got Katie's profile, as she actually lived quite close to the Beacon Hotel.

Indeed, he thought it couldn't be true – maybe someone was playing a practical joke on him. As he was telling me this, Katie butted into the conversation and said, 'I was there at that pub lots of times, but the problem is that when you go to those places, if people are with friends or in a group, no one knows who's available and wanting to meet someone else.' David heartily agreed.

Eventually he plucked up the courage to phone Katie's number but she wasn't in, so he blurted out a message on her answering machine. When she heard it she didn't know what to do, and admitted to having been terribly nervous. Her sister was there and said, 'Well, you'll have to phone him back.' 'No, no, I can't – I'll wait for him to phone me again.' To which her outgoing, full-of-life sister said, 'No, you must return the call. I'll phone him and pretend to be you.' So with no more ado her sister called David.

'Why David ever agreed to meet me afterwards I'll never know,' Katie continued, 'because our conversations after that first one were so different. I literally had another voice – different answers to questions, and of course a completely different personality.' Apparently David wasn't told about Katie's sister until quite a long time afterwards! They decided to meet at the one place they both knew – the Beacon Hotel. 'I knew there and then that I was going to spend the rest of my life with this man,' said Katie. 'I just knew it.'

What David couldn't get over in those first few conversations was that they knew the same people and the same places. He recalled, 'I was completely mesmerised by the whole situation. I had even noticed Katie's father's farm when I was doing some blacksmithing down their lane. I'd said to myself, "That's a tidy farm," and had taken in the location and everything – really just at the time in my life when I felt the most alone.'

Over the months their families met and they all got on well. Both sets of parents were traditional hard-working people who had come through the trials and tribulations that all couples go through and had stayed together. It was a big issue for Katie when the two of them decided that David should come and live with her. As Katie was a churchwarden, and with all parents churchgoers, there were moral issues to be considered. But they both, more strongly than words can tell, felt that this was right, and so they moved in together.

The marriage ceremony was the most magical experience of their lives. Over a second cool drink I was told of the true country feeling they created in everything to do with the wedding. David looked very dashing in a formal morning suit and Katie's dress was designed to represent fields of corn. Their bridesmaids were dressed in similar shimmering deep cream and gold, and everyone carried yellow and cream flowers. Katie walked to the small country church, down a lane crowded with local people, from her parents' home only a few yards away. The transport back to the reception marquee on the lawns was a richly garlanded harvest trailer pulled by a scrupulously cleaned tractor. The wedding feast centred on a pig roast, which suited everyone.

They both told me their love was perfect, but admitted

that virtually immediately after their wedding it was tested because David lost his job. The challenges of married life had already begun: they now had to exist on Katie's salary alone, which made everything very tight and difficult. One night Katie happened to be telling the vicar that life was a bit of a struggle, and before she left he handed her a copy of the parish magazine. That night, looking through it, they saw an advert for the job that David went on to get. 'That job seemed to come out of heaven,' they said, 'just when we needed it most.'

With the new job, a new house was the next thing. They are the first to admit that it isn't the most spacious of properties, but it's cosy and it's their own. As the saying goes, 'New house new baby' and that's exactly what happened. In due course a perfect little baby boy was born.

As I talked to them that afternoon I saw how amazingly similar Katie and David were in so many things – both are blond, and both are of round rather than angular build. Both are emotional people who cry easily. They work hard and have exactly the same values in life, and I suppose you might say they are on the same wavelength. A perfect partnership, then. But would they ever have found each other without the bureau?

2

Little Dolly Daydream

Driving back from Gloucestershire, I decided on impulse to call in at Redditch, the town where I grew up. I knew from my relatives that a lot of the outlying areas had changed out of all recognition with vast numbers of new houses, but I was surprised to find the centre still very much the same as it had been forty years ago. The old-established shops were still situated in a circle around the Green, the hub of the town, and you were even allowed to park in this area still, which I did. I started to walk around the shops and take in the general atmosphere, and as I did so I remembered how it all was so many years ago. I went past the usual high street shops and business fronts, solicitors' offices, hairdressers and estate agents. As I think many people do, when I'm in a different area I generally look into estate agents' windows out of curiosity to see what local house prices are like. As I looked into this particular agent's window I was amazed to see our old family home for sale. Was I right? I'd just glanced across the window, so now I read every detail thoroughly. It truly was – there was no mistake, it was our old house. Immediately I thought that I would love to go and have a look around it.

I took a deep breath, walked in and made up a story that I was moving to the area and would like to view one particular house that I'd just seen in the window. They said they were very busy, and asked if I would mind having the key and showing myself around; it was empty – no one was living in it and there was no furniture. I couldn't believe my luck, as I really didn't want to carry through my pretence to anyone living there. I said I would be delighted, as I fought to conceal my excitement at this opportunity to walk alone around the house in which I had been brought up but had not seen for forty years.

It was very nostalgic to go back to a place that contained so many important childhood experiences and memories. Everywhere seemed much smaller than it had when I was a child. Outside, the garden which I remembered as being so long that it took five minutes to run its full length was in fact only about a hundred yards from end to end. The enormous tree that grew wonderful Worcester apples, and that I would sling my hammock from to the old wash-house, now looked like any mundane tree of ordinary proportions. As I went from room to room vivid memories came jumping out at me. I saw images of scenes that had happened in every corner throughout the many years of family life there.

Our house was in a row of similar ones in the middle of town. When you went up or down the road both ends had much nicer bay windows, with ornate brickwork and welcoming little porches, that made them look exceedingly superior to ours, which was a basic working man's house of the late nineteenth century. There were two bedrooms on the first floor, and a rather frightening large attic stretched over them both. All the rooms except my bedroom had dull, nondescript wallpaper, with doors and paintwork in dark brown. The floors everywhere were brown-stained wooden floorboards covered with home-made rugs.

There was, of course, no central heating and my mother would carry upstairs a shovel full of lighted coals taken from the main living room fire; these would quickly become a small roaring ball of flames in the pretty little black-leaded bedroom grate. Nowadays, if you are lucky enough to have an open fire somewhere in the house you would not dare to balance red-hot embers precariously on a small shovel and carry it about, for one trip or off-balance moment would tip the burning coals all over the expensive fitted carpets.

I was an only child and spent hours alone in my bedroom. I was always short for my age, but well-built and sturdy. My foremost feature was a plump rosy face, and I was always smiling – I am told I gave the impression of having a friendly nature, which I suppose I did have. However, I felt quite shy most of the time. My face was topped by a mass of tight curly blonde hair, a bit like Shirley Temple from the neck up – but, I hope, without the precocious personality that she must have had.

Matchmaking, as I mentioned earlier, was a passion even when I was a very small child, and I always had an unexplainable inner feeling that eventually, given the chance, I would be good at it. My other dream from early childhood was to be involved with farming, to be part of the working life of the English countryside.

Little Dolly Daydream

My room was painted a lovely bright duck egg blue and I spent lots of time here playing with my dolls, as small girls do – or used to before computers and television. One of my very earliest memories is lining up the dolls, some girls and some boys, and matching them up as lifelong partners. The dolls were, of course, a mixed bag. I had one very beautiful Rosebud doll, with auburn curls and a blue checked frock with matching knickers, white ankle socks and shoes with a strap and button. Next down from this paragon were two of a similar nature but missing some items of clothing or wearing hand-knits. Then there was my old teddy bear, a golly and a stuffed dog, a Welsh doll with a leg missing, and several peg dolls. If I was short of partners I used to get a peg from the basket and make someone up – perhaps a dark gentleman with a moustache, or a lady with full red lips. In this way, everyone ended up with someone. Some would be tall, some short, and those with fair hair were matched with other fair-headed dollies. The chatty ones would be put with other chatterboxes, the quiet ones would be paired off together, and so on. I don't remember their characters being more sophisticated or complicated than this.

My father had an old typewriter which lived in the attic above the bedrooms and was hardly ever used. On this machine I would meticulously and laboriously type out the dolls' names and make records of who I was matching them with, and why. When my father went up to the attic one day to type out some letters he found not one piece of paper left, and was so cross with me that I had to avoid him for days.

It was obvious to me, even then, that matchmaking was going to be a lifelong passion. I suppose, looking back on all this now, I could have been considered an odd child in respect of my practice of pairing dolls with one another for marriage; this was definitely not normal for a little girl. Where this obsession came from originally, who knows, – all I can say is that, as was common in those days, my parents were the strongest influence on my life and interests. Most children brought up in the 1940s and 1950s lived with both a mother and a father and, looking back, as was the case with millions of other children at this time, I could not have visualised any other type of life. My parents lived happily together, although there were still remnants of the strain of getting through the war years. Mother and Father married in 1939, just after World War II had begun. They were right in thinking that Father might have to go away, and that is why they married so quickly and so young. For several years he had to work in London without my mother, and then after an accident ended up in hospital for a long time. Being parted like this created little chinks of uncertainty and doubt between them and – as with many other couples at this time, I suspect – it took a very long time to overcome this feeling. But by the time they had got to the 1950s all seemed to be harmonious between them, and their marriage and my life were happy.

I suppose to my young and naïve mind the contentment in their marriage would have made me feel that this was the life for which everyone should aim. That was why I tried to create the same relationships for my dolls, and it strengthened my dream of carrying it on for real people. Now, of course, I am deeply respectful of any style of life that an individual feels is right for them. Many times, talking to someone who is very lonely and feels desperate to meet a partner, I have been known to say, 'You are happy to a certain extent now, although you feel lonely – better to remain that way than bring someone totally inappropriate into your life and end up still lonely and dreadfully unhappy.'

Besides matching up my dolls, which was a good winter pursuit, I used to get enormous pleasure from being outside in any sort of rural environment. I loved to run down through our garden and straight into a vast maze of unused allotments. After the war they had reverted to wilderness and were now full of interesting derelict wooden huts, fruit bushes, apple trees and over-grown hedges that surrounded little squares of land. They had obviously at one time been the allotment holders' pride and joy, and I don't know why they had been largely abandoned. Walkable pathways criss-crossed them, along which you could imagine men pushing their wheelbarrows full of home-grown fruit and vegetables back to their homes. Two or three little streams and ponds had developed, where frogspawn eventually turned into masses of tadpoles.

This land was my salvation from the closeness of my home environment, because I craved space and the open air. I played for hours here, usually by myself but some-times with neighbourhood children. There was a particu-lar grassy spot I would run to, from the house, without stopping. It was the highest point, from which, when I sat down, I could look over a big expanse of open land. Here I could breathe the fresh air wafting from the woods over by the golf course that I could see in the distance.

I would sit on this little hillock for a while and look out over the view. From here I could also observe virtually every patchwork square of the allotments, so if I saw someone walking through 'my land' I would traverse the streams and pathways and weave my way through the hedges to spy on whoever was there. I felt very strongly that they should not be there: it was mine, and I thought no one else knew this ground like me. I'm not sure if that was the case but even now, a full fifty years on, if I was transported back into that maze of hedgerows and trees I'm sure I could find my way back to civilisation, with no faltering or hesitation.

As an only child I did not expect as a right to be constantly playing with others, but learnt different ways of keeping myself occupied. Much of my playing time was spent on my own watching neighbours and visitors to the allotments. Perhaps my practice in those days of quietly surveying adults going about their business helped to build up my understanding of people and situations to give me my matchmaking skills.

Redditch had always been a small industrial town, and in the early 1950s it had not changed much since the war. Although I hated the closed in, grimy feeling when I visited the factory where my dad ran his business, I still found it fascinating. Redditch's main industries at these times were the manufacture of surgical needles and fishing hooks, which Dad processed by means of metal heat treatment. I used to sit in the little office and tidy his desk while looking through into the workshop at the hardening furnaces – three huge fires, open at the front and quite similar to a baker's oven but with a tremendous amount of heat and flames roaring out. Dad would put the surgical needles or fishing hooks in the different ovens according to the temperature required. He used very long-handled metal implements and wore only his trousers and vest but would still sweat profusely with the fierce heat. Steam would burst out into the atmosphere as he put the red-hot needles into big vats of oil to cool – there was a constant smell of hot oil everywhere. Metal heat treatment was hard work, and as it was his own business he would be at it from seven in the morning until seven in the evening every day, except Sunday. The business had been in the family for three generations, so I suppose it was important to him to perpetuate it.

He did not, however, make a lot of money from the business, and so my mother worked from home making fishing tackle. She had her little worktable under the living room window and, using real cat gut, tied tiny, pretty-coloured feathers in different combinations on to little fishing hooks. It was meticulous work, and she had to complete hundreds and hundreds to earn just £2.50 – it took about forty hours' work. And although £2.50 went a lot further fifty years ago, no one could ever grow rich on that kind of income.

I got the idea from my parents that to succeed in life you had not only to work hard but also to work for yourself, run your own business and be in control of your own destiny. It was pointed out that Dad's business had prospects, but that the work Mum did would never get her or any of us anywhere. They were right, because by the mid-fifties my father had expanded the business, buying a new factory and installing massive all-electric furnaces. At last he would not be working so hard shovelling coal into the open furnaces every twenty minutes, a task at which he had been toiling, except for the war years, since he was fifteen. Surprisingly, he had had a private education and had wanted to become a solicitor. But his father would not allow that, and insisted he came into the family business and worked on the shop floor.

Mum was now able to stop doing her fishing tackle job and started working for Dad, and at last our prospects started to be realised. Carpets were bought, our first vacuum cleaner was purchased and I had a new bed. Now that I was older the dolls were consigned to the attic, but not my dreams. As I sat deep in my thoughts on my little grassy spot overlooking the allotments, I understood that the self-employed status was the only one for me. It didn't occur to me then that I could achieve this by indulging the pleasure I derived from matchmaking – I suppose there is only so much a ten-year-old can piece together.

My parents did not share my love of the outdoors – in fact they could not abide the countryside. But my father's father, Grandfather Victor, had given up the family metal business as soon as Dad was old enough to take over, in order to become a farmer. From as early as I could remember I would go to stay at his small farm in the lush, rolling Worcestershire countryside between Stratford-upon-Avon and Worcester, close to a small village called Flyford Flavell. Grandfather Victor was a short man, rotund in body and plump in the face, with a lovely soft unweathered complexion. He would wear the most bedraggled old clothes while doing his farm work, always, as many farmers used to, put together with pieces of string either holding up or wrapped around or entwined through his coats and trousers, which would also be held up with belt and braces, the waist being Benny Hill-style, virtually in line with his armpits. When he went off the farm, however, he would struggle to do up a tight corset put on over his white long johns. As he leaned on the dressing table his face revealed the agony he felt as he huffed and puffed to bring the hooks and eyes together. Massive relief would show on his face in the mirror when the last hook was secured, but I suspect the relief was no more than facial – for any heavy breathing out might have resulted in all the tension dramatically bursting open. Even at such a young age I knew all this exertion was designed to hold his tummy in, but I never knew if Grandfather realised I used to spy on him and watch this fascinating performance through the slit in the bedroom door. He would then don the smartest of suits, accompanied by his trilby hat, and drive off in his famous Jaguar car, and, since he was so short, it looked for all the world as if a dwarf was at the wheel.

My grandmother was an old-fashioned lady. It is awful to think that my abiding memory of her is emptying the chamber pots from under the beds every morning, with a slop bucket and a rinsing bucket that was taken from bedroom to bedroom in the farmhouse. I would spend days helping her gather berries and fruit for her bottling, and sheep's wool to put around her bunions. She would never go outdoors without a large straw hat, which usually had a mass of precariously perched artificial cherries decorating one side. Like Grandfather she was short and plump with enormous arms, which were so good to snuggle down into at the end of the day. I was fascinated by the occasional glimpse of her voluminous shiny pink bloomers that were slightly revealed when she tucked her hanky up one leg. Her modest farm attire was the complete opposite to her going out dress, which would be floral or have white spots on a blue background. With a belt at the waist her large bosom was dramatically emphasised and her hips seemed to span a doorway and a half. She always looked ultra-pristine, sparklingly crisp and clean with a pair of spotless white gloves either worn or carried.

I used to help Grandfather with his sheep, poultry and pigs and would spend hours mending fences, pumping water from old gravity pumps, watching little pigs snuggle together under warm lamps and gathering eggs. I loved the life on the farm and would beg to spend most of my weekends and all of the school holidays there. In comparison to industrial Redditch, it was paradise.

From afar, my mass of curly blonde hair looked like a halo around my head. I was, however, far from an angel most of the time, as I was always getting into scrapes and predicaments when I was staying at my grandparents' farm. Sometimes, because of the naughty things I had done, I would hide for hours in the stable in the top field, from where I could watch the house to see if someone was coming to find me. One of my sins was caused by my passion for tinned condensed milk. I think it was still rationed in the 1950s, but I would run off with a tin to the far end of the farm. With two holes made in the top you could suck out the most delicious nectar in the world.

I was Grandfather's constant companion, and even when I was very young he talked to me about his life, particularly his decision to buy a small farm. He detested Redditch, where we all originated, and got out into the country at the very earliest opportunity. You could tell it was everything in life that he had ever wanted and in my eyes he was always a truly happy man, always laughing and with a smile for everyone. I now realise that Grandfather made an immense impression on me as a child, but I suspect his influence only really nurtured a deep-seated love of space and the open air that may have been in the family genes for generations and had come to the surface with me. Relatives who have researched our family history have told me that we were affluent sheep farmers in Cornwall in the fifteenth and sixteenth centuries – perhaps this could explain my desire for open spaces, to be close to the earth and the sea.

The only time I actually saw Grandfather angry was on the day he was told by his oldest daughter that her husband was about to leave her. His rage was immediately obvious, and he left the farmhouse with his shotgun under his arm to 'kill the bastard'. My terrified grandmother watched him start to walk over the fields in the direction of my auntie's house and telephoned my father, who fortunately was not too far away that day. He seemed to arrive at the farm in a jiffy and went running over the fields in pursuit of his dad. Being the nosey little girl I was, I wanted to witness all the drama. The only way I could get to watch what happened was to ride the small horse, Flicker, that was kept as a pet on the farm and catch up with them across the fields. Flicker and I hid behind a hedge and saw my father disarming Grandfather of the family shotgun a few yards before he reached his daughter's house. My father did not allow that shotgun back at my grandfather's farm for several years.

When I was six years old one of my aunties married a farmer. The farm she moved to was large for those days, centred on an enormous, very old farmhouse with a big duckpond in the farmyard. I would go and stay some weekends and spend my time collecting, cleaning and packing hundreds upon hundreds of eggs. The hens were all free-range and had many fields available for them to scratch around in. The problem was that these fields had lots of trees in them, and one in particular was like a small orchard with apple trees everywhere. Every evening seemed to be spent shaking the trees vigorously or even using clothes props to poke the roosting hens down to the ground, then herding them, clucking, flapping and protesting wildly, into their houses where they would eventually settle down and fall silent. When the milking was finished we would all have supper around the kitchen table – about fifteen of us, family, workers and friends. I relished the talk, all about the countryside and farming.

By the time I got into my dreamy teenage years I used to visualise living on a quiet, isolated farm, working alongside my husband and building a good farming life together. He would be a 'salt of the earth' type and in my young imagination I pictured him as a replica of John Ridd in *Lorna Doone*. I had read the book some time before, and when it was serialised on television I was glued to the screen every Sunday afternoon. My hero was played by Bill Travers, and I fell in love then and there with his strong manly build and brown bushy beard.

I talked and giggled of the future with my girlfriends and described, as young girls do, what I wished for in life. I would explain that my husband would be broad and masculine in build and that we would have lots of children. When I told them I wanted him to be a farmer, they couldn't understand why anyone would want this sort of life. In their eyes sophistication and excitement were surely the main aims in life for everyone, and you couldn't get that by living on a farm. So these rural dreams were quickly knocked off the reality shelf by my girlfriends' feeling that they knew what was best for me.

About this time I started going to the public library in Redditch and bringing back books about matchmaking. I read books relating to the Jewish community and their matchmaking, and about arranged marriages in Eastern countries, and indeed anything else on the subject that I could get my hands on. I suppose that, after pairing up dolls, considering how it was really done in the grown up world was the logical next stage. I was so intrigued by what I felt was the romance of matchmaking, and I remember thinking, 'One day I want to do that.'

I was always interested in people and would read books on the psychology of relationships. And I really enjoyed getting to know others, talking with someone on a one-to-one basis. When I got off a bus, during the journey I would have got to know the life story of the previously unknown person sitting next to me. Looking back, I think my mother used to worry that I got too involved with complete strangers. In the 1950s the dangerous consequences of talking to such people were not anticipated as they are now. Certainly Mother never seriously warned me against it. She just thought me rather odd, I think.

The crunch time for adolescents comes when you really have to decide on your future career, and because I lacked the courage of my convictions I did what my parents wanted me to do. That was to train as a nurse. I did dare to suggest psychology, but that was laughed at as being ridiculous.

Initially I obtained a place to train at the Queen Elizabeth Hospital in Birmingham, but after my interview I realised I would hate being in such a large city and so I decided to go to a smaller place – Worcester Royal Infirmary. It wasn't all work, of course. As soon as I got off duty, especially when I'd been on 'nights', I couldn't wait to go for a spin out in my little black Morris Minor car. On one such occasion I persuaded my two best friends, Jenny and Angela, to join me and we whizzed out to the Malvern Hills. Unfortunately a wheel came loose and we ended up in a ditch, with the three of us receiving minor injuries. We felt pretty embarrassed that morning to arrive back in casualty in an ambulance, on stretchers, exactly where we'd been on duty all the previous night! Before even being discharged from casualty we were summoned to Matron's office and given a severe reprimand and lecture on the perils of motoring around the countryside without any sleep.

My training was very enjoyable, because I loved getting to know people and picked up a lot about how to talk to people in all kinds of situations. I acquired the usual pleasantries of polite conversation which we all use on the surface. But of course, as all nurses and doctors do, I also learnt how to cope with people faced with perhaps the worst traumas of their lives. When you are young you think that life is all black and white, but nursing sick people you learn so very quickly that it is not; there are so many grey areas that we have to accept. Above all, nursing taught me that we are all individuals, each with our own qualities and faults. Little do you realise at the time how these early experiences are preparing you for later life. Without my nursing, I know that my whole approach and attitude to my matchmaking would have been different.

One evening, after finishing work on the wards, I decided to drive home to my parents as I had several days off. It was quite late in the evening, dark, cold and raining. About three miles outside Worcester my Morris

Minor just came to a stop and I suspected I had run out of petrol. There were no houses or a telephone box in sight, so I had no alternative but to start walking back the way I came. It was pitch-black and I had no umbrella or even a jacket. I put my head down and trudged along the side of the road, feeling very cold, wet and sorry for myself. After a while a red car came around the corner and very nearly ran into me, but screeched to a halt a few yards on. The driver got out and shouted, 'Is that your damn car around that corner? I nearly drove straight into it!' I think I was near to tears at this point, and when he heard I'd run out of petrol his annoyance subsided and he offered me a lift to a garage. He then realised he could, after all, be my knight in shining armour and save me from a difficult predicament, and suggested he should bring me back to my car with the petrol. So we made the round trip to the garage and back, he poured the petrol into my tank, made sure it started and promptly asked me out on a date; I married him about eighteen months afterwards.

Mark was a city man, confident and strong-minded, and I think it was these features that attracted me to him. He enjoyed the cut and thrust of business ventures and ran his own garage. I was still working as a nurse, but my heart wasn't in it as I longed to have children and be a full-time mother at home. However, when several months of our marriage had gone by without me becoming pregnant my natural instincts suggested that it would be best to find a fulfilling challenge to take my mind off things. I thought about starting an introduction agency, but I suppose I was still not mature enough to do what I really wanted to do – no matter what anyone else thought. The idea of matchmaking as a serious business in Britain was completely alien at that time. Introduction agencies were considered embarrassing, in bad taste and a last resort for those who didn't have enough about them to find their own mate.

I knew I wanted to come out of nursing, maybe just for a while, but I did want other challenges to come my way, even if at that moment in time it couldn't be matchmaking. Quite quickly after this I recognised a good venture, a business enterprise that to me stood out. I'd heard about a newly built church complex a short distance from where I lived. It had a large hall and about six rooms leading off it, together with a reception area, toilets, kitchen and several large enclosed areas outside, and it was not used at all during the week. I put in a bid for the rent of the premises with the purpose of starting a nursery school. The church authorities agreed and the local council passed my plans. After a few months of getting everything together I opened, and five children were brought along on the first day. A few months after this I was employing five helpers and a trained teacher. Children came from all over the city and it was very soon open all day, five days a week, with a waiting list of seventy.

I had been presented with a lucky opportunity to establish a successful business where there was no competition: private nursery schools in the late 1960s and early 1970s were virtually unheard of. I was twenty-three years old and employing ladies ten or twenty years older than myself. It brought out all the lessons I'd learnt from helping in my father's office, particularly in relation to taking on staff and managing the paperwork necessary to run a business efficiently. Lessons that I did not realise I had been picking up in earlier years came flowing back at this time.

After being offered a very nice sum I eventually sold the nursery as a going concern, invested the money in my husband's business and started working in partnership with him. But at this point destiny shaped my life, and the culmination of events that at the time were very sad slowly turned my life around towards a direction I'd always really wanted. This sadness came about in the ending of my marriage, in my late twenties. Throughout all of our time together we had very much wanted to have a child, but it just didn't happen. Our irretrievable parting came when another woman came into my husband's life who very quickly became pregnant by him. The pain of the loss of him and our marriage, and the child that I so much wanted but that he was going to have by another woman, was so deep, dreadful and despairing that I felt utterly rejected and found myself sinking into depression.

I was, however, lucky in that I always realised my depression was caused by specific events and that it was quite normal to feel despondent and hopeless at such a time, so I never consulted anyone over it. Instead, I tried very hard to see the positive aspects of this change in my life, and decided eventually that the one thing I could hold on to was that now for the first time I could do things totally to please myself. I vowed that I would never again live in a town or city and that I would spend the rest of my life in the country. Jenny, my good friend from nursing days, let me rent a perfect little cottage for £5 a week as she and her husband were going to America for two years. It was deep in the countryside at St Owen's Cross not far from Ross-on-Wye in Herefordshire, a county that I had always loved greatly. I knew so well the mysterious valleys adjoining the Welsh border, where time seems to stand still and where, as you come upon Llantony Abbey, you are taken back into medieval days. You can climb up to the hilltops and explore your way over to Hay-on-Wye and be transfixed at the wonder of such magnificent landscapes, or take pleasure in the architecture, visualising the people who lived here and the events that took place amongst the black and white buildings of the villages in the northern part of the county.

So I moved to the countryside and set about rebuilding my life. The cottage was about half a mile up a dirt track off a quiet lane. The area was called Chapel Tump: apparently in the eighteenth century illegal chapel meetings were held in the garden of the cottage, attended by the good country folk of the area. It was quite extraordinary to sit there and think of the absolute faith and courage that these dissenters had shown all those years ago as they gathered there.

The cottage had an orchard and quite a lot of land where I kept chickens. There were a few cottages a little way off, but no really close neighbours. I loved being there, but sometimes I would go for days without seeing a soul and eventually I became very lonely – lonely for company in general and a 'mate' in particular. For months and months I cried myself to sleep every night, hoping that I would wake up to face a new day with hope and enthusiasm. At times, thinking about my marriage break-up, I reached a pit of despair that seemed impossible to struggle out of. I was experiencing a combination of emotions from shock and disbelief to utter emptiness. Finally, though, I was able to face up to my sense of bereavement. When I talk to people whose marriages have broken down and who are despairing of the future I can say, 'I know how you feel. I've been there – truly I have.' Although it's now over twenty-five years ago, you never forget.

Gradually I became a little braver about life and managed to attend various short and part-time courses at the local agricultural college. I was amazed that after a few months I started to enjoy my studies, and after obtaining some minor qualifications in farm record-keeping I decided to get a place on a full-time two-year course to qualify as a farm secretary. But the course wasn't starting for about nine months and I realised that this would be a good time to get the travel bug out of my system while I had the time to do it. My aim was to return for the beginning of term in September.

I had always wanted to see the Far East, but just to jump on a plane seemed far too easy. I wanted to traverse continents and arrive in India having seen many countries. I got to know several people who were doing this trip around the same time as me and spoke to many who had done it before, and so, loaded with information and promises to try to meet others on the way, I set off. I travelled mostly by rail and stopped in hostels as I went through Europe. Once I'd reached Austria I started camping where I could; if I liked a place I just stopped there for a week at a time. I suppose I looked and acted like a conformist, conservative tourist while in Europe, but when I moved into Asia I realised I needed to rely at times on other travellers and that therefore I should develop good friendships. So I intentionally became a 1970s' hippy in dress, with flowing shirts and a scarf folded around my head (it was good to absorb the 100 degree heat).

In Turkey I fell in love with the country and was amazed at its vastness. I spent days visiting Roman ruins, then relaxed for a week at a time by rivers and waterfalls. It was a real adventure travelling on my own, but I very rarely felt that I was in danger. I did get attacked whilst sleeping under the stars in eastern Turkey, but thankfully the man ran away in fright when I screamed out very loud. I loved going to sleep looking at the night sky, although I'm not sure I would do it now. I still love watching the stars, but with maturity I see so many dangers in this way of life. In some ways it's good that when you are younger you just don't see these risks and therefore do many more things.

By the time it came to travelling through Iran I had loosely joined up with some other Brits. It was good finally to meet people who were older than me – two of the men were in their fifties. Most of the travellers I had come across previously were teenagers who were intent on smoking as much 'pot' as they could. Since I've never participated in this habit, at times I felt a bit out on a limb.

Iran was precarious then, for the Shah was in the process of being deposed and the country was about to enter the grips of revolution. This was completely unknown by me, and my first impressions were of how surprisingly modern Iran was and how stunningly beautiful the city of Isfahan was. The majority of women in the cities in the 1970s wore Western dress, and there was an air of wealth and sophistication. Then suddenly within a few days the whole atmosphere changed. People started to look worried and fearful: very quickly and to our utter amazement enormous tanks started rumbling through the streets and soldiers appeared with guns on street corners. The first time I heard gunfire from the other side of the road was mind-blowing, and I returned as quickly as I could to the hostel where I was staying. By this time our little group of travellers had clubbed together and bought a cheap large vehicle. We thought that maybe the rioting was just located in Isfahan, so we decided to move on south to Shiraz.

When we got to Shiraz, however, the revolution had increased in intensity. After a few days a British-owned hotel allowed us to shelter in the grounds and in some of their rooms. It's strange how very easily you can adapt yourself to listening to gunfire throughout the night, knowing that with each shot someone is possibly killed

– yet you just turn over and go to sleep again. Even when hearing bombs explode you accepted that you couldn't do anything about it. Not all of us, however, were able to take the situation so calmly. One young man whom I met over there, and whom I felt slightly responsible for as he came from my home county of Worcestershire, was absolutely petrified – ghostly pale and constantly shaking.

One night we heard that over three hundred people had been shot. It was then that we realised what sort of position we were in. Everyone seemed to have their own ideas on what to do. Some decided to bed down in the compound and ride it out. Others decided enough was enough – they would journey to Tehran and then fly home. A small group of us decided to get out of Shiraz into the countryside and if possible continue our journey through Iran. It was hair-raising while we were still close to built-up areas and could see conveys of tanks filing into the city. But we tried to stay low and insignificant most of the time and camped in some wonderfully beautiful and remote spots overlooking the Persian Gulf. In some ways it was like paradise to wash in clear, warm rivers, eat fruit and nuts you'd just gathered from a tree and lounge in the sun all day with the azure sea glistening in front of you. And all this while a revolution was going on!

Eventually we decided to try to travel on into Afghanistan and to do so we drove north, away from that beautiful sea. For about five days we journeyed through unbroken desert, passing nomads in colourful flowing clothes. But my roaming and exploring came to a sudden halt when my friends and I found ourselves in a very dangerous situation in Afghanistan, with another revolution in full swing. Gunfire and tanks were all around us once again, and I for one had had enough. The two older men and myself had always kept enough money aside to be able to pay for a flight home at any time (I suppose that really does differentiate me from the true hippy). So in the end, although we stuck it out for several days thinking it would subside, we caught a plane back to Tehran and then another to London. I got home regretfully, without finishing the trip I'd planned to India, but at least I was safe.

After a week or two of getting used to sleeping in a bed again and not ducking and diving from tanks and snipers, or looking for insects in my shoes in the morning, my thoughts turned to what I was going to do until my farm secretarial course started. I decided to take temporary jobs that appealed to me and would take me to various parts of Britain, my only condition being that anywhere I worked would have to be in the countryside.

I saw an ad for a job in Staffordshire: a person was needed to get all the bookwork up-to-date on a farm and to look after two small children while their mother was in hospital. 'I think I could do that,' I said to myself, and was offered the job immediately when I applied. This was my first excursion to live in the north. Little did I know that I would never return to live in Worcestershire or Herefordshire and that I would learn to love another part of England just as much.

I knew this job would be good experience before I

started my course. It was a bit daunting, though, as the farm books had remained untouched for so long. The children were sweet and I greatly enjoyed their company. Their grandmother would come to take over from me on my days off, and I always tried to spend those days away from the farm. Staffordshire surprised me with its diversity, and I made my first acquaintance the desolate, windswept moorlands in the north of the county. It was on one of those days off that I decided to attend a local farm sale.

I looked around but, as sometimes happens at auctions, the catalogue contained misleading descriptions of some of the items and I couldn't get interested in any of the lots. My car was parked quite a long way off and suddenly the heavens opened. Luckily, I was able to duck for cover in a nearby shed. As I dived in I glimpsed a man also sheltering from the unexpected downpour. We spoke, of course of the dreadful weather, and gazed out at the rain which was deafening as it beat down on the corrugated roof – which itself was leaking badly, so we stood there with coat collars turned up, still getting soaked. We started to discuss the auction, and then he asked me about where I was working and a bit about myself, and we passed the time as sociably as we could under the circumstances.

He said he lived near Bakewell in Derbyshire and very often came back Staffordshire way as he'd been brought up in the locality and knew it well. I told him I'd never been to Bakewell but understood it to be a lovely market town. 'Come over,' he said. 'Let's meet up and I'll show you around.' He asked for my telephone number, and as he wrote it on his sale catalogue I looked up into his face for the first time. His coat collar fell aside and revealed a bushy brown beard! I was transfixed; then, as he turned to leave the shed, for the rain and eased off, he said, 'By the way, my name's John. What's yours?'

I couldn't even utter a goodbye to him, as I was rooted to the spot with an overpowering reaction in the pit of my stomach. A quiver shot down my spine and I thought, 'What's happening?' Here, in the middle of the Staffordshire moors, in a muddy, wet cowshed, I had bumped into the image of my romantic adolescent dreams – John Ridd himself. I thought I must be dreaming.

But I wasn't. John contacted me a few days later and suggested he drive out to where I was and we'd have a drink at a local pub (I thought the idea was for him to show me Bakewell, but never mind). Now I could really look at him for the first time, as I hadn't paid that much attention or indeed been able to see him clearly in the dingy shed. He was tallish, with a kind, appealing smile and a mass of brown curly hair. His glasses added character to his roundish face, he was broad and masculine – and he had that fantastic beard! I suppose I was going through the same process as anyone meeting a prospective match via the bureau for the first time.

He said he was an avid reader, so we talked to each other about the books we'd read. I asked him what his favourite book was, and that same overpowering reaction came tingling down my spine again when he answered, 'Well, if you consider all the books I've ever read, I'd have to say *Lorna Doone*.' Every word he said was so uncanny and seemed to suggest that providence had caused us to come together.

We had a really lovely time together that evening, and when it was time to go our separate ways John asked if he could see me again. I was delighted. A dairy farmer who looked like John Ridd and made my stomach turn somersaults – what more could I ask? I was about to suggest that we might meet up the following Saturday, perhaps for a picnic, when he said, 'Of course, I'll have to get the hay in before I can see you again, so it may be a week or two, depending on the weather. I hope you don't mind.' Well, what could I say? And thus began a lifetime of playing second fiddle to a farm.

John was a very decisive man who, when he made his mind up over something, did everything he could to get what he wanted. Within a short while he asked me to marry him. One evening he asked me twice and on a particular Sunday he asked me three times. I have to admit it wasn't too romantic. He said he couldn't 'court' me over the winter, as being a livestock farmer he would be very busy then. 'Our relationship will never last over these months with you so far away at college. And with me working all the hours I have to I'd never find time to see you,' he said. 'Marry me now – soon, before winter. September will do.'

I still intended at that stage to take up my place at agricultural college, but realised I had to make this big decision quickly. Yes, marriage to John would give me the lifestyle I had always wanted, but that shouldn't be the most important consideration. The top priority has to be the person you are marrying. And, of course, when you have had one marriage end and experienced the utter grief that this brings, you don't want to go through it again. But I did say yes, and I've never regretted it – and I never did take up that place at college.

John and I hadn't known each other a long time before we decided to get together. I remember being very apprehensive: had I really made the right decision? As I packed up my possessions at the little cottage my mind was whirling with a mix of emotions from elation to fear: where was I heading? But, on the other hand, I've always looked on life with great optimism and believed that chances are for the taking.

The sun was streaming through the little orchard that surrounded the cottage and shining on the paving stones just outside the front door. I'd virtually finished packing my things in boxes and I'd put the garden furniture away, and so, to have my final cup of tea in the sunshine, I had to sit down on the floor leaning on the closed door. I thanked this place for being my little sanctuary. It had sheltered me from the world that I had not wanted to face for a while, and gradually its peace and tranquillity had healed my wounds and made me able to grasp with enthusiasm my life ahead.

As with most farmers, all my possessions were loaded into the horsebox and transported up to the farm. When I arrived, knowing there was no going back, I did feel like a bride in an arranged marriage. I didn't know John too well, but I knew that this would be my life from now onwards and that it would work and that we would be happy. We were married on Michaelmas Day, before winter set in – a traditional wedding day in rural life.

Having settled down to married life together we decided quite soon to start a family. If only it was as easy to make a baby as it is to say, 'Yes, we'll have one.' After a year of trying, still nothing had happened. We went into a period of temperature-taking, medical consultations, tests, infertility drugs – we investigated them all. Eventually the consultant said, 'Just go away and forget about making babies for a while.' He advised me to do something challenging, interesting, something that I'd always wanted to do, to take my mind off it all, and as I drove home I thought hard about his advice.

John had recently employed two young lads to help with the farm work. He had always done his own book work and felt he wanted to continue doing most of it himself, so there wasn't much I could do on the farm. That evening I sat at the kitchen table weighing things up and thinking about what the consultant had said. Gradually my thoughts came together and my resolve hardened until I found myself shouting out loud, 'Yes! I'm going to do what I've always wanted to do – I'm going to start a marriage bureau just for farmers.' I was shocked as well as delighted to realise that I could realistically consider fulfilling my lifelong ambition – and very grateful for the fate that had made it rain that day on the Staffordshire moors.

3
The Farmer Wants a Wife

That same evening, after John had finished milking, I told him about the consultant's advice to do something interesting and challenging. Then I waited until he'd finished his meal and settled down to be comfortable before taking a deep breath and telling him of my plan to start a matchmaking agency for farmers and country people. To be honest, he just fell about with mirth and amazement. 'A dating agency! Eh, Pat, my darling, it 'll never work, farmers using a marriage bureau! Eh, you'll not get farmers doing anything like that, never in a million years.'

I hadn't expected immediate agreement, but after my success with the nursery school I was a much more determined lady. I knew I could run a business well and I knew I was still passionate about matchmaking. And in fact it didn't take long for John to realise that it would probably be a good thing to do and to admit that, if anyone could make a success of such a venture, it would be me. That was good enough. It would have been great to have had more enthusiasm, but never mind – to get his agreement was enough for now.

That was in the autumn of 1981. By the early spring of

1982 I had planned how I would do the matching of couples and prepared a business plan. I borrowed £50 from the farm account to pay for my brochures to be printed. To this day John still jokingly reminds me that I've never paid it back.

I can still remember the look on the printer's face when I presented him with my first brochure design and a mock-up of the registration form. He was an old man who I think had never, ever come across the concept of a marriage bureau, so he couldn't grasp the idea at all. Tentatively I submitted by post the wording for an advertisement in the *Farmers' Guardian* newspaper. When I telephoned their office to enquire about the cost they said they would have to think about it, as they had never accepted an ad like this before. So then I approached the *Farmers' Weekly*. Very quickly I was told they would not accept such 'personal' advertising. Was I an escort agency? they asked. They probably thought I might be even worse: was I on the game? They didn't put it into actual words, but after the conversation I had with them I know they were thinking about it. To my great relief, after two weeks of consideration the *Farmers' Guardian* accepted my first ad. How odd all this seems today when you see all the deeply personal ads in the papers!

The only other specialised agency in the country at the time was one in London for Asian people. There were a few other general agencies, virtually all based in London, but you could literally count them on one hand. Dateline was the biggest and Heather Jenner's Marriage Bureau was the longest established. There was, however, no one specialising in country people.

I could have surreptitiously sent off for brochures and forms from these agencies but I purposely didn't do that, as I wanted to do things my way and not be influenced by others. To me it was so important that farming and country people had questions posed and methods of matching developed to suit them and their particular way of life. I felt general agencies could not possibly take into consideration the unique and very diverse aspects of a country lifestyle.

Before anyone joined the bureau I conducted several trial runs on matching people up. Would their education be the most important factor? Or background? Or type of work? Or age? I realised quite quickly that I would never be able to state in absolute terms the single most important compatibility factor. But with most, I thought, it would be location and age. There were no personal computers then, of course, so my basic office equipment consisted of a phone and a typewriter and carbon copy paper. My fees in 1982 were £20 for eight introductions. Wow! Those were the days.

I crossed my fingers in the last week of May 1982 when, on the Friday, my first ad came out. At lunchtime on the Sunday I had a phone enquiry. Could they have a brochure? And before I knew it, over the following week I'd received numerous enquiries. I quickly sent my brochures out and in June people started sending in their registration forms and joining the bureau.

All new businesses need a bit of luck, and mine came in

the way the new members joined. They could all have been either men or women, or with no age group being represented twice to give any chance of a match. They weren't, however. People in their thirties were the most common, and amazingly the sexes were roughly even in numbers. Very quickly I was able to match people up, write to them regarding each other and complete my first introductions. I couldn't really believe that I was at last fulfilling my long-held childhood dream.

In some ways it felt wonderful to be doing what I had always wished to do, but, as with everything that you have waited a long time for, I thought the bubble would burst. John couldn't quite understand how thrilled I was to be matchmaking; in some ways I think he just humoured me and felt it would all come to an end soon and I could move on to something 'proper'. Of course, he would never say that: he says he learnt early on in our marriage to keep quiet at the appropriate times. It's so different from the sort of work he could cope with that he cannot imagine anyone else loving it.

Quite honestly I thought I would only run the bureau for a short while until I became pregnant. Then, I had no doubt, I would close it down and concentrate on family life. However, eventually John and I had to face up to the fact that we weren't going to have our own children, no matter how hard we or the doctors tried, and we decided to acquire our family through adoption.

In 1982 the most lovely little two-year-old boy was placed with us. Matthew was gorgeous and lovable, enjoyed outdoor life and the farm, and immediately became the most precious person in our lives. By the time he had been with us for two years we applied to adopt again and, having been accepted, were all set to complete our family.

At the time Matthew was placed with us we were told that he had grandparents who loved him dearly and were inconsolable that they would not see him again. When he was five years old, a few months after my own mother had died, the thought of his natural grandmother kept coming to the front of my mind. Surely for her to be able to give her love once more to Matthew couldn't be bad. I resolved to find them.

Through my research I was able to trace them and one Saturday afternoon, hoping I was doing the right thing, I telephoned them. 'Do you have a grandchild called Matthew who was given up for adoption?' The response was at first silent disbelief, then, 'Yes, yes, we do.' The following week we all met up in a local hotel and they spent several hours with Matthew and us. We all had lunch and they played with him most of the afternoon, while we looked on and got to know them better. You could tell they adored him – he was their only grandchild, and they admitted it was a dream come true. We parted company promising to keep in touch and meet up again soon. One week later to the day, our darling little boy drowned in an accident on the farm.

How can anyone describe the utter despair you feel on losing a child? You want to stop living so you don't have to feel the immense and unbearable pain. You want to die to be with your child – you don't want him to be alone.

John and I were were numb with shock, and whilst we still didn't believe what had happened the ambulance men wanted to take him away. They couldn't take him away without us, we said. Wherever he went, we would go too. We wanted to be with him, to keep him warm, to put our arms around him and love him. Maybe, we thought, we could even breath new life into him – but you can't.

By about two o'clock in the morning neighbours and friends had persuaded us to go to bed. John and I lay still clothed, with our eyes open, for hours. I suppose eventually we dropped off to sleep, but at such times the worst comes when you wake up in the morning and just for a moment you're convinced it was all a nightmare. And then your devastation is rekindled when you realise it's all true.

My old friend Jenny and her husband came and stayed. Another neighbour insisted on staying night and day for a while, so wouldn't be alone. But John and I needed to be alone together. We needed to hold each other and comfort each other, knowing that only each of us understood the other.

We all know the inevitable process that you go through when arranging a funeral. On Monday afternoon, two days after the tragedy, it suddenly dawned on me that Matthew would need something nice to wear. He was so young, and he really did look like a little angel. I asked a friend to buy some material so that I would be able to sit and sew something pretty for him.

Tuesday came and more things were organised. For the first time I thought about his grandparents. Whatever would we say to them? How could I bring myself to tell them? But I did. I phoned them and said we would like them to attend the funeral as members of our family. They agreed.

I finished hand-sewing a gown for Matthew to wear – yes, it was a labour of love and every stitch was so very special to do. The funeral day came and the church was packed with village people and friends. Matthew's natural grandparents joined our family, and the social workers who had seen us through his adoption were there too. All this support gave us the strength to carry on and get through the day.

> A little boy so sweet and true,
> With gold blond hair and eyes of blue.
> Full of mischief, problems few,
> Oh my love, how we will miss you

Matthew's little grave is in a corner of the cemetery where other children are buried; some of them he even knew.

The difficult time starts when all the formal rituals are over and you have to start living again. Up until then, I have to admit, I didn't cry a lot. I did cry, of course – but not like John, who wept much of the time before the funeral. Afterwards, our roles reversed and I went into an agonised decline. I cried incessantly and couldn't bring myself to do ordinary things like answer the phone or even go out. The one thing that pulled us both through it all was that we clung to each other. I would come across John slumped in a chair weeping silently, and I'd put my arms around him. He would find me crying as I was peeling potatoes, and he'd comfort me. Neither of us became badly depressed. We were utterly sad, but there was a reason for this and together we gradually got through it.

We made ourselves take regular days away from the farm together, and started to talk about the future. Matthew's natural grandparents visited us regularly. We would talk about him to them and show our many photographs. All this made our marriage stronger, and we felt able to cope with anything we might have to face.

So, with time, we came to look forward again, and we adopted a robust and smiling little baby boy, whom we named Ben, when he was a few weeks old. Just under two years after that our pretty daughter, Sarah, then five months, came to live with us. The first visitors to come and see our new babies on both occasions were Matthew's grandparents, and of course Ben and Sarah grew up to call then Grandma and Grandad. Throughout the years they have spoilt our children and loved them to bits.

When Matthew was placed with us I decided I should start to employ staff to help me. Thankfully I had a part-time secretary working in the bureau when Matthew died, but my best friend Jenny, from the days when we were training as nurses together, just stepped in and took over all the organisation. She said I was not be concerned about it at all until I felt ready to come back. Fortunately at that time in her life she was not nursing and could therefore do it, but even so she was a wonderful friend to take it on at all.

My first full-time secretary was Anne, a local farmer's daughter who was wonderfully versatile and adaptable. The arrangement was that at any time I needed someone to look after the children while I was in the office she would babysit as well. Anne concentrated on the admin work, and I did all the matching of couples and client interviews. By the time Sarah arrived in 1987 I had taken on my second secretary, Mary.

Life in the summer of 1987 was hectic. I had two children under two years old and the bureau was getting busier as each month went by. The only time I had to myself was if I got up early in the morning at the same time as John, who got up to milk at 4.30 a.m.

At this early hour I loved to walk down the farm drive and through the lush fields close to the house, although I would always keep the house in sight as the two babies would still be fast asleep in their cots. The fields would be heavy with the grass that would make our silage crop and feed our cows throughout the winter. There is nothing more wonderful than that early morning birdsong which nearly deafens you as you walk through the trees: the complexity of sounds would almost take my breath away. Those walks would rejuvenate me for the day's work, which would be full of the complexities of dealing with people and their longings to meet someone special, bringing up two small children, running a busy farmhouse and organising the local toddler group. I needed to breathe in the beginning of the new day with its distinctive freshness and watch the sun slowly creeping above the horizon. As I did so I would think of the joy of having such longed for children, and I would declare to myself and the woods and fields that life was good.

As I walked back towards the farmhouse I would look over to the east where some of the glorious valleys of the district lie: Lathkill Dale and Bradford Dale, with their limestone walls skirting rocky outcrops, dotted with trees and speckled with grazing sheep. Our home surroundings were pretty wild, too. Had I been a casual passer-by wandering past our garden in those early summer days, I would have been totally surprised to be told it was cultivated at all. Farmers aren't good gardeners, I think mostly because they haven't got the time and also are possibly not over-inclined to spend hours tending a few fancy flowers when they could be growing things for money just over the wall.

In those busy years in the mid-eighties I used every available hour to work in the bureau office. Often, if after my early morning walk the children were still asleep, I would try to take advantage of the situation and start work early in the bureau office – I could always hear any awakening sounds on the intercom, which had been wired through.

I used to advertise that the office was open from 6 a.m. every day. Operating that way, I found many farmers would telephone me before they started their day's work. I suppose it was unusual in those days to have an office up and running at this hour. Now, of course, people can make contact on their mobiles, at any time of day while doing anything, even driving a tractor, so I don't offer the sunrise service any more.

My bureau office is in the old stables of the farm. All the buildings in the vicinity, in the Peak District of Derbyshire, are of grey-white limestone with corners, window edges and door surrounds in honey-coloured sandstone. They have the old sandstone roof tiles, and of course all the limestone is beautifully weathered and mellow with a few creepers and patches of aged moss. The stables are about a stone's throw from the farmhouse across the farmyard, which is not the muddy, dung-filled area that it would have been a hundred years ago but a clean square tarmac expanse more like a modern-day small car park. The farmyard is bordered by buildings on three sides. One side consists of the farmhouse, the second an old traditional barn and the third the old stables. They were used to house poultry for many years after the horses disappeared, but were still always referred to as the stables. Not long after I opened the bureau I realised that this would be the perfect place to have my office. In the transformation we only used half the stables and kept as much of the character of the place as possible. Three rooms were created, and the old wooden beams were left exposed in the ceiling whilst some of the walls have been left as original stone.

The first room you walk into is the one in which I interview clients. If contains two snug and cosy high-backed velvet armchairs in a deep warm rose colour, and a pretty country-looking settee with matching curtains. All four of the plain cream walls now display masses of large photographs of successful introductions. There are also two large tables set against the walls, covered with smaller, gold-framed wedding photographs. This room also houses an old desk at which I take notes when I'm talking to clients who come for an interview. Through the window I can look down through the farmyard to the front field and the farm drive.

The other two rooms are the true working rooms where the office equipment lives, including storage for hundreds of profiles, maps and the paraphernalia needed to do the matching. I have always considered these offices my little domain, and, although of course they are usually shared with a secretary or two, it's where I have always loved to come to have time to myself.

When I'm sitting in the office, I suppose I must look like a stereotypical homely, comfortable and, I hope, friendly farmer's wife. I am still that short, rounded person I was as a little girl, only now more so as the years have advanced – a bit like Dawn French, so I'm told. My round face still has a rosy complexion, even though my blond curls of yesteryear have been replaced with brown mid-length hair – still naturally curly, and always wispy and windswept, making me look as if I've been dragged through the proverbial hedge backwards.

I have to admit I'm no longer the timid, shy person of my childhood days. I will approach anyone and say anything which I think needs saying. I have a serious, compassionate side to my personality, but I certainly laugh a great deal and take a very optimistic and light-hearted approach to life. I delight in seeing the funny side of everything we all do, but I have to admit that I'm a bit slow to get jokes – or so John tells me. Usually I have to have a joke explained twice to me.

I'm accused by my friends of being slightly eccentric. I don't understand this at all, but they seem so sure that I am. I suppose I just do what I feel is right at the time. It doesn't bother me if others don't follow or don't agree with me, although I'm always adamant that everyone should be respected for their own individual point of view, and I suppose more than anything I enjoy oddness and individuality.

I tend to wear feminine, flowery and full-skirted clothes and tops, but on days when clients visit me I always put on something smart with heels and do the very best I can with my wayward hair. Little does anyone know when they meet this reasonably well-dressed, proficient-looking woman that I've possibly been dressed in the most undesirable garb you can imagine earlier that day while doing something unbelievably mucky on the farm.

On one silaging day in 1988 I got out my big, very muddy pram, which I kept just for pushing the children around the farm, and on the wire tray underneath put the men's lunchtime snap. (This is a Northern word for a working man's food and drink that he has during a break from his work.) Two or three baskets and bags containing tea, cups, cake and so on were tied to the sides. It was incredibly cold that summer day, so I wore a very old overcoat that was totally threadbare but very warm. It was so ancient that all the buttons had come off, and the only way to fasten it was with a complicated series of lengths of baler twine. All this was put on over a quite presentable dress, as I was expecting a client to come to the office for an interview in the afternoon. The whole ensemble was completed with the essential wellies. I had planned that, when I got back, the children would have their afternoon nap and Anne would babysit over at the house while I interviewed the client. The food had been taken up into the first field and as I was turning the corner on my way back to the farmyard I caught sight of the client – he'd arrived early! Alighting from the biggest and poshest Mercedes I had ever seen was this figure dressed in an immaculate suit with matching tie and pocket handkerchief – I think he was the smartest person to arrive in our yard, ever. I ducked back; he couldn't possibly see me like I was. You couldn't have told the difference between me and a bag lady that afternoon.

Once he had been invited inside the office by Anne I tried desperately to get my overcoat off but I could not undo, come what may, the dreaded baler twine – I felt like a trussed-up chicken trying to extricate myself from this massive garment. I realised I had to get to the house and cut the strings with a knife, but the only way I could pass the office to get there without him seeing me was to duck as low as, or even lower than, the pram and push it past the office windows. I could see that Anne was keeping him talking with his back to the window – but then he turned quickly and, Anne told me later, his face was a picture of absolute amazement as he caught sight of this pram with two laughing children travelling under its own steam past the office window. Thank goodness he didn't take a closer look to see me, head down, knees wide apart like a demented wobbling duck, hanging on to the underside of the pram handle.

A quick slitting of strings, kicking off of wellies and brushing of hair resulted in the presentable professional lady he had come to meet. Anne took over the children in the house and I settled down to interview him with complete aplomb. It turned out that he had a large farm in Cheshire, and it was his mother who had sent him to me. She had probably had as great an influence on his choice of clothing that afternoon as she had on all his other affairs, because he promptly brought out a list of qualities that Mother wanted in his future wife. The lady had written down ten points that without any deviation whatsoever needed to be present in a daughter-in-law. I asked him if he really wanted to find a special person to share his life with – honestly and truthfully without Mother being there. Well, no, he was quite happy as he was, it was just that Mother wanted grandchildren so much. I'm afraid I had to send him on his way with a pep talk about having the courage to tell Mother exactly what he wanted in life.

On another of those early summer mornings I was reading through a registration form from a man named Andy who lived on the Cumbrian moors. As he was not a dairy farmer with cows to milk I assumed he wouldn't be an early riser, and left my call to him until a little later. When I did so I thanked him for his registration form and asked, really just to make conversation and learn a little more about him, why after being alone for so long he had decided to try to meet a partner.

'Something just clicked in my head one day,' he said. This broad Cumbrian accent made me visualise a salt-of-the-earth man with maybe quite old-fashioned clothes and with a few days' stubble, as I knew he had lived alone for a long time without any female influence.

'What do you mean?' I asked.

In a slow, thick voice he described how on his forty-ninth birthday, exactly twenty years to the day since he had come to his farm, he had decided that he wasn't going to continue with his life as it was. He wasn't melancholy in his conversation with me – quite hearty and jolly, in fact, cracking a joke mostly at his own expense at what his mates would say if they knew he wanted a woman. He would never live it down and he'd have his leg pulled constantly.

So often, of course, the 'I shouldn't really be doing this' attitude covers acute embarrassment or desperate shyness. I think with Andy it was total embarrassment. He was facing the fact that his lack of feminine company was important to him. In the macho world that many men inhabit, their friends and workmates can control so much of their lives – unknowingly, through their joking and sneering they condemn someone to being utterly lonely.

Andy said he would like to come for an interview at the office, so I told him we needed to make an appointment.

'Well, it'll have to be in September when I come down for Hartington sheep sales,' he replied.

The picturesque village of Hartington, about three

miles away from us, is renowned for its village pond, the cheese factory making Derbyshire Stilton, and the annual sheep sale which people attend from all over the country. He said he came to the sale every year, and he'd looked me up on the map and realised I didn't live too far away. So I asked him to give me a call when he knew exactly when he was coming down, and then put his form aside. I was confident I would see him in September, when he would combine the business of trading sheep with finding a wife.

I looked down the field and saw an army of tractors and machinery coming up the lane leading to the farm. All in a convoy like a disjointed green caterpillar possibly a quarter of a mile in length, they rolled up the drive and parked themselves up on the front field. No wonder John was happy today. The silaging team had arrived.

Silage has taken over from hay on most farms in Britain. Haymaking still takes place, but only to a very minor degree compared to years ago. One advantage of silage is that it can be harvested more quickly than hay. You don't have all that tedding and turning for days on end, only for the stuff to be rained upon – with the result that you have to start all over again. Unlike hay, silage doesn't need particularly sunny or good weather when it's cut, and it can be handled and stored very efficiently. Most of all, it has a better nutritional content than hay and is therefore highly beneficial, particularly to dairy cows. Sadly, it smells different from the glorious waft of newly made hay, but you just have to accept that old methods have gone and new ways of farming have taken their place.

Yes, the silage contractors had arrived, and I knew full well that word would get around the farm instantly, as everyone would have heard the noise as they approached. Quick as a flash our farm workers seemed to have left whatever they were doing to come to the front field and walk round all the appliances and equipment and calculate how much everything had cost. Every year they announce how much more wealthy the contractors have become. On hearing these figures the contractors always deny them in tones of complete disbelief, claiming that they are not a penny wealthier but certainly half a million more in debt! Some farmers buy their own silage equipment and do it themselves, but more and more employ contractors. They do actually come with larger and more efficient equipment every year and the job always seems to take less time than the previous year. It used to take six or seven and sometimes eight days to cut and gather our 200 acre harvest, but with their newer and larger systems it now takes only two days.

It's exciting when the contractors arrive, as our usual routines are disturbed and there are new people for everyone to talk to with news to catch up on. It can be stressful for John, though, as he wants his silage in quickly. But if all is straightforward and the weather is kind, then it's a good and happy time. Our contractors have been visiting us for about eighteen years. Usually nothing except a breakdown stops them from working from early morning until dark. They never stop except for ten minutes to eat from their own snapbox, which they bring from home, or when I take out supper.

That morning, just as all the men were gathered around the newly arrived contract machinery, Lynda arrived in full view of our men and the contractor's men. She had been working for me for eighteen months and was ravishingly attractive. The sway of her hips and her swishing long hair stopped every man in his tracks. The contracting men, who had not seen her before, stared mesmerised as this gorgeous creature swept across the farmyard. And then came the comments: 'Got a new woman for me, Lynda?', 'Are you on the books, love?', 'I think I'll part exchange the wife.' A few weeks earlier there had been a day we shan't forget easily. John and the farm workers were concreting a small portion of the farmyard as Lynda alighted from her car, and all their eyes were diverted to her alluring figure. The concrete went everywhere it should not have gone, followed by a lot of clearing up and the invention of explanations of how it had happened.

Lynda had come across every single variation on any comment a man could come up with, and took it all in her stride with a laugh. Unknown to the men, she had brought a quality of toughness into my office. You wouldn't for a moment guess that this beautiful and desirable woman was my mainstay when it came to getting in money that I was owed. Of course she had other attributes that I appreciated – quick typing skills and an understanding of country life, as she had been brought up in a remote Peak District village and married a local farmer's son – but most of all she could cut a person dead on the phone with her expertise at getting them to pay their bills. No one would realise when they looked at her long chestnut hair, angelic face and petite figure that I valued her for her ruthlessness. The problem that I've always had is that I'm an old softie and would always be taken in by a sob story – Lynda wouldn't.

Despite the arrival of the silage contractors that morning, the normal office routine still went on. 'Well, what do we have here?' I said aloud to myself as I turned from Andy, my Cumbrian sheep farmer, to what looked like a very different client. I smiled as I read through Jane's details. She had written that she wanted to meet a gentleman farmer – he must not work, but must have enough leisure time to take her out whenever she wished, and her main aim in life was to be able to organise his hunt balls! He should be tall, dark, handsome, very romantic, wealthy, with a large country house, and preferably be the local Master of Foxhounds. It seemed to me that she wanted a cross between the simmering passions of Darcy accompanied by his baronial country estate, the good looks of a young Nigel Havers and the social and hunting connections of Prince Charles.

For a moment I contemplated my own luck if I were to encounter such a man – tall and handsome, with all the brooding sensuality of Darcy, riding out from his grand mansion. I envisaged him daydreaming of meeting a dumpy, plump, pink, round-faced, middle-aged lady like me, picking me up as if I weighed no more than a feather, and carrying me away on his white charger for hours of rapturous lovemaking on the shore of his shimmering lake.

Then I realised I'd got to get back to the realms of reality. I thought about how I could gently let Jane into the secrets of the facts of this world. There again, Pat, I said to myself, never prejudge and assume she is a plain Jane. She could have the body of Liz Hurley, the connections of Camilla Parker Bowles and the sexual expertise of Madonna. How wealthy she was I suppose would not matter if she fulfilled all men's dreams with these combined attributes. I telephoned her, carefully went through the delicate tip-toeing sequence of finding out about her real situation in life, and started to explain that gentleman farmers hardly existed nowadays but if a glut of them did happen to live close by her luck would really be in. Her connection with the countryside was that she had been brought up on a very small farm as a child. Her marriage had broken down, and she had been left with three children all just entering their teenage years. Her only income was the maintenance cheque from their father. 'When the kids are driving me mad, I switch off from them and fantasise about my dream man,' she told me. After a long and difficult discussion we came to an understanding that she would leave the choice of her introductions in my hands, but, sadly, the Master of Foxhounds never did turn up for her.

As I walked over from the office to the farmhouse I remembered I'd got to get supper for about twelve hungry men. Before I started I made myself a cup of tea to relax a little from the day's work and think about what I had in the pantry. As in most old farmhouses, the pantry in ours is as big as any normal room, and the old stone slabs to keep the food cool are still there. The farmhouse is about two hundred years old – not very ancient, considering that many of the farmhouses in the locality are twice that age. It's detached from the other buildings around the yard and looks like a typical Derbyshire cottage in that it's double-fronted with a central front door, elevated slightly from the yard at the top of a flight of old stone steps. Shrubs have been planted beneath the windows that flank the door. Years ago, when the cows trailed through the farmyard to be milked in the shed, you would never have been able to grow pretty flowers in their pathway as they would have been immediately devoured as the cows sauntered to their milking appointment. However, times have changed and farm animals no longer roam anywhere and everywhere.

Mere Farm was so called because up until the late 1950s it had no mains water, and all the water for the stock came from large man-made ponds called meres, located around the farm. Meres, which are completely round and drop quickly to about six feet in depth, are lined with clay and for centuries were the only source of water on the limestone farms that lie high above the rivers in the valleys. The main mere for the farm was directly at the back of the farmhouse, virtually lapping at the door of the old dairy. After it was no longer needed it was filled in, and it is now a circle of concrete encircled by a border of pretty flowering shrubs. The children loved riding their bikes around and around it when they were young. We do still have several other meres around the fields which act as water sources for the cattle, but everywhere also has mains water laid on.

Even on hot summer days my navy blue Rayburn still rumbles on, so I went and put a joint of meat in it to cook slowly over the next two to three hours. The kitchen is long and includes a section for sitting in comfy armchairs with newspapers constantly strewed about, and a big central pine kitchen table which has chairs around for six – several more chairs for visitors' use stand against the walls. John always sits at the top of the table in the chair that his father left him, and I always use the small Windsor chair his mother gave me when we married. Around the Rayburn at the top end of the kitchen are the work units housing the hub of the kitchen. Most of the ceiling, which is not at all uniform, consists of black beams, and two of the walls are exposed limestone. It's not a picture-book, glossy magazine-type farmhouse kitchen but a very livable, warm, functional hub to our home.

The back entrance leads into a room that houses what look like all the wellingtons, boots and shoes, for the population of our local town, coats for every season, sticks, flea sprays, sheep-marking sprays and odd implements whose function that would confound any mind. I guarantee you could make anything from the collection of bits and bobs you will find in this repository – you name it and you'll find it here. Leading off from the back entrance is a room where all the men wash their hands on coming into the house.

I ferreted away that day, finding jars of chutney, pickles, cakes – anything and everything that hungry men would eat in several hours' time – and started putting it all into big wicker shopping baskets to load into the back of the truck. Finally I found my huge old teapot that would soon dispense gallons of tea to all and sundry. It has rested for several years next to a brand-new sparkling tea urn that I refuse to use. It was my Christmas present from John one year. 'An urn?' I exclaimed. 'How can anyone with an ounce of romance buy his wife a tea urn for Christmas?' A hurt expression came over him. 'But I thought youw'd like it,' he said, totally disbelieving that I could long for anything more appealing.

When I went to pick up the children from the school bus I called in at the village shop for the bread. I made a lot of sandwiches and packed them up with sausage rolls and pasties and other filling foods. I took tea, coffee and cider to drink and loaded all this into the back of the pick-up. At silage time all the men stop at the same time and get together to eat. They would always joke with our three farm workers, and Ben and Sarah would often show off their skills driving the quad bike, with the dogs following. Every year, it seems I'm feeding the five thousand, when in fact it's only about a dozen.

Tom, the boss man, usually gets off his tractor first and presents himself at the back of the pick-up for supper. When his workmen see this I suppose they feel they can do the same. It's great that they have been coming for so long that we feel like old friends and can go straight back into last year's conversation where we left off. This year Jo, the oldest man in the team, started to wind up his boss. He claimed he wasn't pulling his weight – but with a smile on his face. I suppose he can say anything to Tom, knowing full well he can get away with it after the years of work he has given him. There were hints from one and all that Tom was surreptitiously going behind the wood for a sleep. I suppose any busy contractor working virtually day and night, in the peak of the summer, would give anything to have a sly sleep – but he just can't. Jo puffed on his pipe and took great pleasure in stirring up matters. He then told me about the latest child that he and his wife had fostered over the year.

By this time Tim had arrived – the buck raker or man who deals with all the grass once it has been brought to the silage pit. A quiet and serious man, Tim is always lovely to talk to and a good worker. Keith appeared, munched on the beef sandwiches and said he was starving. His machine picks up and chops the silage, and he is very particular about his straight and exact lines. Big beefy Brian eventually joined us from where he had been mowing a few fields away. He always appreciates the food and says so. Others appeared who were doing the carting, and with our own men and John and the children there can sometimes be up to thirteen or fourteen individuals standing or sitting on the grass, drinking and eating around the truck.

We've enjoyed these picnics in blistering hot weather. At other times it has been so cold and windy that it seemed more like January, and I have produced a huge pot of stew or even gone to the local fish and chip shop to feed everybody. Usually it is just pleasantly warm, and by coincidence the feeding stop is in a part of the farm with glorious views over the surrounding landscape.

When the silage team have moved off to another field I always try to go over to one of my favourite spots on the farm and sit in front of a nice, good little wood. (I wonder if other people find some woods sinister and eerie and some good and kind and peaceful to be in.) This wood is always nice and comfortable. Over on the western boundary of the farm is Arbor Low, a prehistoric stone circle where people buried their clan folk about five thousand years ago. Directly in front of me to the south lies the old Roman road that led from Buxton to the south. How many soldiers would have marched along there? To the left I can see undulating and pockmarked fields where lead mining took place about two hundred years ago. How strange that, in this isolated spot 1300 feet above sea level, life has continued for generations upon generations and the lives of the people throughout those five millennia have been so diverse. In this enchanted location I always feel dwarfed at the immensity of the human experience.

4
The Perfect Match

As each year passes I find more and more people get in touch in the first place because they have been encouraged to do so by friends who have either had success with me or know someone else who has. This is great because straightaway they have a positive attitude towards the bureau, knowing that it works. But most people still get in touch through seeing my advertising in farming and country newspapers and magazines or on my website.

Occasionally someone who married through the Farmers and Country Bureau several years ago will telephone to report that the marriage has now broken down. This is a very sad situation, but I suppose if one-third of marriages end in divorce, some of my alliances too will eventually come to an end. Sam from Devon married through me about eight years ago. When he phoned a while back I immediately sent my memory back over the years, located him in my mind and enquired gushingly, 'And how are Liz and you?', only to be told, 'Liz and I divorced a few months ago. Things became difficult when her son from a previous marriage started to get older and my agricultural employment agency got busier. But we did have five good years together and I'd like to try again, if you'll have me.' In some ways I feel pleased when they revisit me – not pleased, of course, that they have gone through the trauma of divorce – but pleased that they don't feel it's my fault and that they feel I can help them again.

A new way through which some people have got to know about the introduction agency in recent times is advertising in doctors' surgeries. It only happens in very isolated parts of the country, where some doctors now realise that severe loneliness can be a contributory factor in both physical and mental illness among rural people. Recognising this fact, the practice administrators have requested small posters to put up in the waiting room and brochures that can be handed to anyone who they feel would benefit from contacting me.

Tony, from Northumberland, contacted me through a recommendation by his GP in 2000. On the telephone he told me about his depression, and then decided to come to the office for an interview. I was so pleased about this. I didn't feel I could go ahead and accept his membership if I hadn't met him, as I was concerned that his depression was too advanced. When he did come to the office I learnt that his wife had died three years previously of breast cancer. He had a close and loving family, but each year since he had lost his wife, another son or daughter had left home for university or to further their career. His depression had got worse and worse and he couldn't stand the thought of eventually being completely alone. He cried in my office as he told me about the last few years of his life.

I said I wouldn't let him meet anyone for about three months, but asked him to try to put himself on an even keel and get mentally stronger before I gave him his first introduction. In his case, I said, I was not aiming at a serious relationship to begin with, as I do for most people, because I felt it was important for him just to get out and start meeting new people. He needed to enjoy new friendships, discover new places to visit and generally to develop a new life for himself in the company of others. Tony agreed to try to get the better of his depression, and his last words on going out of the office door were, 'I feel better already, because you're giving me hope.'

Tony and the first lady I introduced him to went out several times. He told me he got as much pleasure from looking forward to going out for the evening as he did from the actual going out. He even joked with me on the phone about how he felt like a youth again, getting ready for a date, dressing up and wondering what she would be like.

Janet was the second lady he met, and he really started to enjoy her company. Never married and in her late forties, she was a career woman from Newcastle-upon-Tyne but had always lived in the countryside. She told me how much she enjoyed the company of his children. They weren't constantly at home, but they seemed to accept her in their father's life and she loved the family atmosphere. She also told me how different she was from his domesticated late wife, and that this was possibly what had got them off to a good start. She arrived at the farmhouse one day to find Tony making jam: 'I wouldn't have a clue where to start,' she told me. His wife had done all the farm paperwork and the housework and wasn't an outdoors person, whereas Janet loved being involved with the farm. On her days off from work she enjoyed driving a tractor or helping with stock. It was good that his wife and Janet couldn't really be compared. After about a year of going out I was informed that they were planning their future life together and Tony said, 'I've never looked back or had really bad depression since I met Janet.'

Sometimes people like Tony aren't actually ready for an introduction, even though they feel they are. Possibly they have recently gone through a trauma in their life. Often their previous partner has left them or they are widowed and just cannot bear the thought of being alone in the immediate future. They feel the solution is to join an introduction agency quickly. In some ways it's only because that previous marriage or relationship was so good that they cannot bear not still being part of a couple, and want to replace the lost relationship quickly. I talk to them in a sympathetic and understanding manner, but I explain they will never recapture what has gone. Only when they have faced up to this and looked on their next relationship with fresh eyes are they ready to continue with meeting more people.

The opening line I have heard most frequently when someone telephones me is: 'I've never done anything like this before.' Twenty years ago people were far more embarrassed to join an agency than they are now, when it's definitely getting more acceptable to meet others in this way. We would all like to meet someone special casually and naturally, fall madly in love and live happily ever after without the involvement of a third party. But, sadly, that perfect world is not for everyone. When people request a brochure over the telephone, some of them are very businesslike and order it as they would a travel catalogue. The other extreme give you their life history in the first two minutes and want to know everything about the agency instantly. I've had parents (usually mothers) requesting brochures for their sons and daughters, bosses asking for the brochure to be sent to their employees, and daughters asking on behalf of mothers or fathers. Sometimes I will get a brochure sent back to me in the post with words such as 'I don't need this' written across. I assume it has been requested by some friend or relative thinking that they know what is best, but obviously do not.

Some people, as I've explained, come to the office for an interview. I can't force people to do so, because many live hundreds of miles away. Wherever they come from, it can be very difficult to drop everything and travel to see me, and I do realise that some people find the prospect of sitting in front of me for two hours or more totally daunting. I do feel I make the interview a pleasant and rewarding experience, but of course we all have preconceived ideas!

I must admit I love doing these interviews, and I cannot believe my luck in life that I can regularly get to know a complete stranger on a one-to-one basis. Many people say they have never before been able to talk about themselves, completely, for such a long time. One of the most important things I do is ask the person to describe, if they met someone special, what they would like their life to be like in three years' time. This is very revealing and really does help me in getting to know a new member, for although the past can be important and the present certainly is, it is vital to put two people together who are looking for the same things in life in the future.

I give advice where I can see it is needed or requested. For some people, simple matters can be the hardest to tackle. What do I wear? Where do we go? How to behave? What to do? and a hundred other queries. I always talk about all these as sensitively and thoroughly as I can, and of course everything is completely confidential.

One day I had back-to-back appointments. I had just cleared my desk and was reading through the notes on my next client when there was a tap at the window and there stood a cyclist just taking off his bicycle clips from his tweedy trousers. He was also wearing a flat cap and a checked shirt. 'Now what?' I thought. 'Not another lost tourist.' In the event it turned out to be my next interviewee. He had no car and his brother needed the farm vehicle to take some stock into market, so he had decided to cycle from West Yorkshire to keep the appointment. 'My God, it's a long way,' he cried as he got his jacket out of the carrier on the bike. Indeed, it must have been a hundred miles or so. Once he'd put the jacket on you would never have known that he'd just cycled that incredible distance. I was in awe at such dedication to see me.

At times I do see very shy men and women, but usually it's the men who are the more apprehensive gender. They describe how they would just die at the thought of making a romantic approach on the phone to a lady they didn't know. One man had a very pronounced stutter, so I suggested he wrote to her. I tell men that most women are delighted to receive a letter from a man, as this lovely way of communication is rarely used nowadays.

I remember I had great difficulty with one man because he felt he couldn't phone a lady as he was so shy, but he couldn't easily put pen to paper either. I told him that I would help him write letters, so long as when he eventually met the girl he would tell her the truth immediately. So he told me what he wanted to say and I duly wrote the letters for him. After about three months the crunch time came when they had to meet. I was so nervous for him, as I'd really got to know and like this man while helping him with his letters. Amazingly, all went really well, and they quickly decided to tell everyone that they had met at their local vet's. Actually all must have gone very well indeed, because they are now happily married and have two children.

Sometimes it's better not to take someone on or to fill them with false hope when I know they will eventually be disappointed. I've had to do this when I've known full well it's going to be very difficult to match them with someone. This might be because they live in a difficult area or are of a difficult age. It's always a hard decision to make, because you can judge after speaking to a person on the phone whether the thing they want most is the hope of meeting a partner. So sometimes, even if I think their chances of meeting someone through me are slim, I say I will keep their details just in case someone comes along. But I don't actually register them, and of course I return their payment. In this way I am under no obligation to give an introductory service, which would be very difficult to achieve – but it does keep their hope alive.

Once a person says they wish to join the bureau a profile is completed, which consists of a description of that person from what they have said about themselves in their registration form. Then the matching process begins. Of course, before you go into the finer points of matchmaking you have to get the basic factors right. Location and age are the first considerations, then you look at their smoking habits, marital status, religion, children they might have or wish to have, educational background, personality and compatible aspects in relation to country life. Once I've found about three or four registration forms that seem suitable matches using all these basic points, I go on to judge the finer points, such as a liking or not of pets, horses and blood sports, type of holidays preferred, politics, interests and hobbies. The individual preferences that you personally know about the individual through interviewing them or talking at length with them on the phone are taken in consideration, and then last but not least their hopes for the future – the type of lifestyle they wish to lead. Do they want to change career, move to another part of the country, expand their farming business, be part of a family? So many aspects to consider. Often, there is a very obvious match that stands out from the rest when you have thought about everything, and the choice of one person to match with another becomes obvious.

When I've decided on the particular match letters and profiles are sent to both people, who are asked to reply either by returning the letter or by telephoning the office to indicate if they wish to go ahead or not. Of course, most people phone as they want to talk to me about the prospective introduction. They usually ask, 'Do you know any more?' which invariably I don't, as I always put all that I can disclose in the profile. With a 'yes' from both, each other's first name and telephone number are sent out on the same day and the man is asked to get in touch with the lady. She will be expecting a call and, with these preliminary obstacles well and truly overcome, you hope all will go well.

To report on whether introductions were a success or not some clients write back to the office with reams of description of how it all went. Some, on the other hand, give the briefest of comments, such as 'good' or 'no good'. Others call in and offer a complete run-down on typical misunderstandings such as confusion with car parking. So many times over the years I've been told of couples who were planning to meet at a pub but didn't know that it had two car parks. One driver would wait in the front, say, and the other in the back, each thinking that the other had not turned up. Finally they would go home, destined never to meet.

I've been told of men forgetting their wallets and fumbling about in the car to find an odd pound or two so that when they walk with their introduction into the pub they can at least buy her a drink. Sometimes ladies get totally lost driving to a location and I've had distress calls: 'I'm completely lost – help!' One gentleman from the Channel Islands, on the other hand, would fly his own helicopter to the lady's location and pick her up to fly on to wherever she wished to go. I've had train spotters take a lady out for the day, thinking she would take great delight in their favourite activity. 'Never, never, never again,' has been shouted more than once down the phone line. And then of course I've heard from ladies who have been told, 'Just got to nip back to see a calving cow', only to spend the rest of the evening ankle-deep in a cold, muddy field bringing forth new life.

One lady, a schoolteacher in her early thirties, planned to meet up with her introduction for the first time at half-term – 'So it didn't matter about getting back home too early,' she said. When they met, they were instantly, completely and absolutely besotted with each other. She decided to return to his farm that evening, and whatever came to pass made her decide not to return home for a week. I am pleased to say they married at the end of term.

I've had people telephone me from the pub toilets to say, 'He's awful! How do I tell him I don't want to see him again?' I tell them to say, 'It's been so nice to spend the evening with you. I'm really pleased we met, but I don't think we're suited to a long-term relationship.' This is why I stress that no one should give away their full name and address until they are sure they want to go ahead and see the other person on a regular basis. But so often, even if you know you aren't totally compatible, it can be nice to remain friends. A good friendship, after all, can be just as valuable and rewarding as a more personal relationship that doesn't work out.

5
Go Forth and Multiply

Sometimes, as I sit in the office and pin forms together, I ask myself if it's my skill that actually joins these two people together or whether everyone has a destiny all set out for them. When I first read through a new registration form I try to understand the specific written picture of that person. It's easy to put everyone into a cliché category: the workaholic farmer, the horsey woman, the would-be country gent, the village odd job man, the doggie lady, the greenie, the typical farmer's daughter. But no one is wholly what you think. Another exercise I do when reading a new form is to assess how easy I feel it will be to find a partner for this person. I've had people who would be very difficult to match up – in fact I've nearly said to them, 'Sorry, I can't help you', just to have fate tell me that I don't know everything, for, to my complete and absolute amazement, they have found success on their first introductions.

There are some basic factors I always look for when thinking about difficulties, such as a short man or a tall lady. If you are a man under five foot eight inches your chances are radically reduced, as ladies so often want to meet tall men. There seems to be a higher percentage of men prepared to meet a taller lady than of ladies willing to meet a shorter man.

Up until about thirty-four years old I always get more men than ladies who wish to join the introduction agency; after which the ages seem to level off. Once you get into the middle forties far more ladies approach to join, as there are so many of them unattached in their forties and fifties. Maybe it's because, when a marriage ends as the couple are heading towards fifty, the reason is so often that the man has found a younger woman. Older men often feel they don't need anyone to help them find a partner – they can do it by themselves, they say. Sometimes they can, but in reality farmers and countrymen frequently fail to meet the right woman by themselves.

A high percentage of my first introductions are success-ful and the clients never come back on to the register, but to achieve that you've got to come up with someone the likes of whom they haven't met for years in the course of their own lives. We may call this luck, but is luck the final result of the destiny that was planned anyway?

There was only one occasion when I was absolutely positive that the two people I put together would actually marry, and I was so confident I think I would have taken a bet on it. Edward had joined my bureau about a month before and, unusually, I had interviewed him at his market garden home in Oxfordshire. When Elizabeth came to the office for her interview, she had only been with me for ten minutes when I said, 'I know who I'm going to introduce you to, and I think you'll be married within a year.'

'But you can't say that! How on earth can you say that?' she replied. I agreed that it was a ridiculous statement to make, but I felt very strongly in my mind that things would turn out so. About nine months later, when I had a stand at the Royal Show, Edward and Elizabeth came to see me on the showground and told me of their forthcoming marriage. I must admit I did feel that destiny had taken a hand with them. About four years ago they brought their three lovely blond-haired children to visit me at the farm.

But the path of true love doesn't always run smoothly. September arrived and with it Hartington sheep sale. I remembered Andy from Cumbria, who had spoken to me on the phone and said he would combine visiting me for an interview with bringing some of his sheep down to sell at Hartington. He telephoned me on the first day of September to say he would be down in a few days' time and wanted to come for an interview.

'I don't know what time I'll get to you – it depends on what I sell,' said Andy. 'I'm bringing down a lorry full.' I looked through the office windows many times when I suspected I'd heard a lorry coming down the drive, but he must have been delayed. Then, when I was totally immersed in some introductions, I jumped a mile when there was a knock on the office window. No one had driven into the yard so I didn't think I'd got a visitor, but yes I had. A man was standing outside gesticulating that he wanted to come in. He announced himself as Andy as he stepped through the door and took off his cap.

'Andy, how on earth did you get here? I didn't hear your lorry.' I was quite bewildered – it was as if he had been dropped from the sky. Where was his lorry?

'I left it at 'artington,' he said. 'I didn't want anyone to see me lorry coming down your drive. They might 'ave thought I was after a wife, so I've walked over t'fields – that way no one can see me.'

I smiled to myself. Well, this was a first. That someone had traversed the three miles of walls, valleys, moorland and woods between us and the sheep sale, on foot, just in case, on this darkening evening, someone might happen to see his lorry turn up our drive and just happen to know the vehicle – when he must live at least two hundred miles away! This determination definitely warranted a successful match.

Andy was a tall man, over six foot, and had quite a mop of grey hair. It was very thick and bouncy and sort of stuck out from his head, horizontally, before and after he took off his cap, which was strategically placed on the side of his head at a very acute angle. He was broad and stocky, a bit weighty, with massive hands. He was in his market clothes, for him possibly the smartest he would wear year in year out – green waistcoat and tweedy jacket with working brown trousers and boots. I asked him to sit down, poured the usual cup of tea and asked him to tell me about himself.

'Oh! bloody 'ell! Nobody's ever wanted to know about me.'

'Well, I do,' I said.

He heaved a deep sigh and began his story. 'Well, like I said to you before, I decided to do something about myself way back in June. When I got up one morning, I looked in the mirror and said, "God it's been twenty years since I've been here."'

I encouraged him to carry on. 'Been where – what did you mean?' I asked.

'You see, me wife and I moved on to our farm twenty years ago. I was twenty-nine and she was twenty-seven years old.'

'Tell me more, Andy,' I said, as he had dried up a little. He constantly seemed to think that one sentence sufficed as a description of his whole life. 'I really need to know a lot more about you,' I urged.

'I couldn't believe it. One day she was there and the next she was gone. Taken all her stuff. We'd only been married just coming up for three months. We moved in the week after we were married on 5th April, my birthday. I bought the place and took it over on Lady Day. She told me she found the place was difficult to live in. Leading up to the wedding she knew I was going to buy the place and what the farm was like and that it was going to be hard work. I never really knew after that what was the trouble. She just left without telling me and I never saw her again. I found out she was all right because she would send her mother letters – but not to me, not once.' After a pause and much twisting of the cap in his hands, which he had kept resting on his knee, he said, 'I don't ever talk much about this sort of stuff, you know.'

'I can understand that,' I replied, 'but you need to tell me about the time straight after your wife left.'

'Hell – it was just like hell. I just sat. I'd do what I had to do with me stock, but that's all. I suppose I just survived – but it was the shock of it all, you see. I just couldn't believe it. I've never talked about it to anyone like this in all those years. I keep myself to myself, you see, to do with these sort of thoughts. My family were brought up to get over things, so I've never even talked to my mother in all these years.'

I told him it was best to try and talk about deep feelings so that he could put it all behind him and start afresh. Gradually he went on.

'I'd known her many a year before. Then we started going out when I was about twenty-five. Up until then I was too busy trying to get started by myself. Dad had a small farm, but I was determined I was going to get me own place. I started me own flock when I was seventeen and every year got a few more and rented more land. I've always been a dealer as well. It just came natural, like. When I saw the farm up for sale I knew straightaway that I wanted it. I got together as much money as I could and applied for a mortgage. With all that in hand, it seemed only natural to ask her to marry me. It was a quick wedding, but we'd known each other for years.'

I then asked Andy if he had ever gone through a divorce.

'Ah, yes,' he said. 'About five years after she left I had letters from a solicitor telling me she wanted a divorce. I just signed everything and it was all over. Best thing really.'

All of a sudden I saw this large masculine man, confused and trying so hard to understand how all that he had described could have happened to him. Since he had been alone he had devoted himself to making the farm successful. He had paid off the bank loan and had accumulated more acres and a large breeding flock of good sheep. His dealing had spread far and wide through Cumbria, Northumberland and the Pennines.

After a bit more conversation I was pleased to see him start to relax, and we agreed that I would start to look straightaway for a suitable lady. After a couple of hours, he departed as he had come – silently and stealthily, like the Black Magic man of the night.

Over the next week I set to searching for an introduction for Andy. I thought she would have to be a down-to-earth woman, someone very familiar with farming. I came across Beth, who lived in Yorkshire, and sent Andy's details to her. Very quickly she phoned back with the comment: 'He's a bit too upmarket for me. All this hunting, shooting and fishing – he sounds like a country gent.' Just as I was about to explain that he wasn't like that at all, she said, 'But my friends think I should have a go, no matter what, so I will.'

The next day I had another interview in the office with a male client. I make it a rule not to answer the office phone when I'm doing an interview, but that afternoon my secretary was off sick so I had to cope with both. It was Andy replying to the profile of Beth that I had sent him.

'I'm glad I've got hold of you. I'm stuck inside doing paperwork this afternoon because the job I was going to do I needed my neighbour to help, and the awkward bugger said he'd got to go out somewhere. Anyway, yes, I'll be introduced to her if she wants, but God, does it have to be a Yorkshire lass?'

'What's wrong with Yorkshire?' I exclaimed.

'They always know their own minds too well. I'm sorry, I suppose I just can't see this sort of thing working for me. And I'm in a bad mood because Dick's had this day away and I hate paperwork.'

I put the phone down, concealing a small, wry smile, and returned my attention to Richard who had been waiting patiently.

For a month there was complete silence from them both, and then one day Beth telephoned. I said how nice it was to hear from her and asked how things had gone with Andy.

'Well, I never really believed it would work. In fact, I thought it would be utterly hopeless. To be quite honest, I really didn't think anyone would be interested in me, but the thing is – we're getting on very well. We're very similar in our ways, and each time he comes over to me things get better between us. Of course, each time he comes he brings his wagon and usually goes out and buys some sheep so he doesn't have an empty journey going back. But that's all right. Next time we meet I'm going over there. So we'll see how it is then.'

What a wonderfully down-to-earth, practical, tolerant woman, I thought to myself as I put down the phone.

As the weeks went by, the next one to telephone was Andy. 'Eh. She's a cracker of a lass, she is.' He then went silent and I sensed he wanted to talk, but couldn't quite get it out. Eventually he told me that Beth was going to stay the weekend at his house in a few days. I said that seemed a good sign and asked what he was worried about.

'It's been so long, you see,' he said. 'You know what I mean. It's been a long time since I entertained a lady – what will she expect?'

I then realised that for a straight-talking Northern man to discuss 'entertaining' meant that it was getting a bit too much for him – he was huffing and puffing a bit by then.

'Andy, it's like riding a bike – once learnt never forgotten. It will all come back to you, mark my words.'

A little time went by before Beth telephoned me again and started the conversation by explaining that she had something really difficult to cope with, to do with Andy. Then she went on to say that she now knew why Andy's wife had left him. My mind raced on and I dreaded whatever I was going to hear next – could it be a voracious sexual appetite? With a lump in my throat I said, 'Why, Beth?'

'It's that house! I've been to some run-down places in my life, but I've never seen anything like it before. And Andy says it was just like it is now when they moved in on their honeymoon. There are no floor coverings anywhere, just stone and bare floorboards – and even then there are floorboards missing all over the place. The windows are open to the rain and wind, and the wall-paper just hangs off the walls. No wonder his wife left him! I put my foot down and refused to visit him again if I have to enter that house. So he's said he'll buy a caravan and we can do our courting there. The thing is that I get on with him so well. So I'm not going to let this damn house get the better of me.'

Beth's practical nature did win out in the end. Six months latter she telephoned me to say the old house was being demolished; they were having a brand-new one built and would move into that together. She said that they had gone into it all and had an architect do the plans. The local planning authority was so pleased that the eyesore Andy called a house was being pulled down that they had readily passed the plans. 'It'll be a wrench for me to leave my smallholding and friends in York-shire, but I love the man and I want to be with him. Anyway, I've put my place up for sale – so there's no turning back.'

When I'd complimented her on her success and told her he obviously just needed a woman like her, I put the phone down feeling so euphoric that I raised both hands in the air and shouted, 'Yes, I did it!' It never varies. Whether I'm alone or with someone else in the office, whenever I hear of another successful match I raise both hands in salutation of my great satisfaction in finding love and happiness for another couple.

I'm often invited to visit couples who have got together through the agency. A visit of this kind is a very satisfying and happy occasion, and I like to turn it into a short holiday for myself, perhaps visiting friends or family as well. About a year after I'd heard from Beth I was invited to visit Richard and Mary, who also lived in Cumbria, and Jessica and Hamish, a couple in Scotland who had telephoned and mysteriously said they had a very big surprise for me! So I planned a trip to see my friend Angela in Scotland, stopping to see the others *en route*. Angela and I had been friends for many years and were rarely able to see each other these days, so occasionally we met up in a nice hotel where we could be pampered and catch up with all our news. It seemed ironic that when she, our mutual friend Jenny and I were all nursing she was the one constantly making the nursing blunders, yet she had stayed in the profession and climbed the ladder. Now she moved around the country while advancing her career.

After leaving the motorway I drove over the high fells of the Lake District to the farm, which I had been told was very isolated, with the closest neighbour about a mile away. When I arrived they both greeted me warmly, and over a cup of tea I started to tell them about Jessica and Hamish, whom I was going to visit next. After about five minutes there was a knock at the door and Richard and Mary started giggling and smiling, announcing that the surprise had arrived. To my absolute amazement, in walked Andy – the Andy who had visited my farm with his cross-country SAS tactics about a year before. I looked at him open-mouthed and managed to ask him whatever he was doing here.

He edged into the room and there behind him,

grinning broadly – in fact everyone was grinning broadly – stood Beth.

'You'll never believe this, Pat,' said Mary. 'Andy and Beth are our next door neighbours! Andy and Richard have lived side by side here on the Cumbrian moors for twenty years!' Mary went on to explain that she and Beth had got talking, and found out that Richard (Dick to his friends) and Andy had both been members of my bureau for many months – next door neighbours who worked together most days and talked about everything under the sun, but never dreamt of telling each other that they were seeking partners through a marriage bureau.

The news eventually sank in and they went on to tell me even more.

'Do you remember,' Richard said, 'that I came to your office for an interview? Well, that day I was supposed to help Andy with some farm work, but I told him I'd got to go out for the day. I really came down to see you in Derbyshire.'

Andy followed by reminding me that he'd been a bit annoyed that Dick had gone off for the day, but little did he know when he telephoned my office and I gave him Beth's telephone number that Dick was actually sitting there by my side! We all fell about with mirth and amazement at this coincidence, and they were all for opening the whisky and making a party of it. But I still had to get to Scotland, so I had to refuse.

Beth and Andy insisted that I see their new house before I left, though, so we cut across the field and there it was. It was really lovely, and certainly no expense had been spared: I could tell another happy ending was in sight. They even looked alike – country faces blooming with health, round, ruddy, extremely down-to-earth. Andy's face was covered with embarrassed smiles, and as I looked knowingly back at him I felt certain that his long-forgotten skills had come to the surface without too much difficulty.

But the day's surprises were not over. I got back into my car and started my journey further north. I was heading for a hotel at Ballater, not far from Balmoral. This journey worked rather well, because only about 50 miles away from Balmoral I intended to break my journey to visit Jessica and Hamish. I knew they had been married about two years. I'd not met either of them before, but I found this surprise they had in store for me very intriguing. It couldn't be another neighbour, could it?

When I arrived at their farmhouse it looked about a thousand years old. It was built of dark stone, maybe granite, and stood there like an enormous fortress surrounded on three sides by high grassy slopes, with the huge farm buildings at the back. Jessica greeted me at the door and seemed so pleased that I had arrived virtually to the minute that she was expecting me.

'Oh! I'm so pleased you've arrived on time, because Hamish has left combining to come down to meet you for a little while before we have something to eat.'

Hamish arrived virtually straightaway and, as I always do, I took a really close look at this couple. The most striking aspect of Jessica was her beauty, with her pale skin and black hair. I understood immediately how Hamish could have fallen for this exquisite woman. He was broad and masculine, with a full head of auburn hair and very blue eyes, and they made an extremely attractive pair.

I started to ask about their lives before they met, and Hamish described the reason why he had never previously married – he had just not met anyone and never really stood a chance, because he had always worked such long hours, had always lived on his remote farm and had always been quite shy. Jessica had lived all her life in a village about twelve miles away but had never known Hamish. She had been married before at a very early age, but she and her husband had grown apart, not had children and divorced in her mid-twenties. 'Life was rather dull then, and really for the next ten years I did nothing with my life except work,' she added. Jessica told me how she and Hamish had decided to get married about six months after they had met. Some of their close family thought this was too soon, but the two of them could see no point in waiting as they were getting older and wanted to be together.

They both then apologised for not being in touch since their wedding, in the small, white local church. Then they looked at each other and laughed and said how busy they'd been in the last year. 'Anyway, come with us into the kitchen to see the surprise we've been keeping for you,' said Hamish.

I followed them both into the farm kitchen, and after Hamish beckoned me to come to the far end of the room my eyes moved to the right-hand corner. I really couldn't take in what I was seeing – there before me were four babies about a year old, all playing together, laughing and smiling in a big wooden playpen.

'This is our surprise – this is what has kept us so busy over the last year. These are our quads born just over a year ago, and they're all boys,' Jessica proudly announced.

To be honest, I think this was one of the biggest shocks I've received in my entire life. Staring in total disbelief, I uttered, 'Quads, quads, I'm responsible for quads, for quads!' and we all laughed together.

At last I recovered from the shock and asked them if they had had fertility treatment. 'Oh! no,' Hamish proudly announced. Then Jessica coyly admitted that the babies were soon on their way – two or three months after they were married she knew she was pregnant. One by one a cry, a shout, a noise and banging came from four individual babies, and it was time for them and us to have our meal. Each was put in a high chair; Mum had one each side of her and Dad had one each side of him. The babies were helping themselves very much to their own dinner, but with continual help from Mum and Dad. I just couldn't keep my eyes off them all.

Hamish had to go straight out after the meal to continue with combining, but he gave me a great hug and some flowers and a big photo of the babies sitting together in a row. 'When I joined your bureau and you introduced me to Jessica, never did I imagine how my life would change. Somebody up there decided I'd had it too quiet for too long and said, "Let's change his life completely" – but thank you, Pat.'

So for the next hour I helped give each one of these lovely little babies their afternoon bottle before they settled down to a sleep. Jessica told me she did normally have help with them, but today they had wanted to manage alone in order to have some privacy with me. The boys were all bundled into a massive big black pram that looked a hundred years old, two one end and two the other. Jessica explained that it was the farm pram which she allowed to get dirty, but for going out to town they had specially adapted buggies that slotted together. She pushed the pram out and we walked around and then over to my car before I left Jessica standing by her big pram waving me goodbye, with her four babies fast asleep.

When I returned home after a week I rushed up to John and said, 'You'll never believe what I've got to show you!' He didn't know anything about my journey up to Scotland, as we don't usually speak to each other when I'm away – I've always found it nicer to catch up on everything together when I get back. I produced the photo of the quads and said, 'What do you think of that? Just look what I'm responsible for. Isn't it wonderful? Four little babies, quads born to the farmer and his wife I visited in Scotland.'

John looked at the photo in silent disbelief, shook his head sorrowfully, and said, 'Good God, woman, do you realise what you've you done to the life of a poor unsuspecting bachelor?'

6
What's for You Won't Go by You

Whether it's fate, luck or good business that brings people together, more often than not the first thing that attracts is appearance – you see someone and fancy them. Then, depending on the strength of the attraction, the boldness of the people involved and all sorts of other incidentals, words might be exchanged, meetings arranged, and there you are with a relationship. But if people can't meet the right type of potential partners easily, because they aren't living close by, how do they ever meet? There is no doubt that introduction agencies provide a unique and valuable service, especially in these circumstances, for many people. They provide golden opportunities which would otherwise have been missed.

Instinct made me pair together the most unlikely man and woman – a comedy actress from London and a sheep farmer from a remote Scottish island. This couple had to surmount all sorts of obstacles even to have their first meeting – different personalities, work commitments, parental wishes, not to mention a distance of 500 miles between them! There were many false starts, hesitations and doubts along the way, but it was an exciting journey of discovery for them both. This is their story.

Mary had a successful career on the stage and TV and working as an agent for comedians in London, but she knew her career wasn't going to make her happy and she wanted to get out. She attended Quaker meetings, and during the quietness of one of those meetings she realised that the only thing that would make her happy would be to get married and have children. So she decided to set this course of action in motion. Her parents had a farm on the slopes of Snowdonia, and she really wanted to go back there. All her friends knew she wanted to live in the country, and one in particular had made a television programme on my bureau so she had some good background information. Mary decided to join up. She decided there was no reason to put all her eggs into one basket and she wasn't going to set her stall by it – it was just an interesting chance.

She told me, 'There's nothing more disappointing than going out with someone for a few months, and then him saying something like, "Oh, of course, I can't stand children." In normal circumstances you skirt round issues like that because you don't want to put people off. Quite often I found I was dating people with all sorts of hidden problems and unresolved issues – they didn't know what they wanted. I was becoming sure about what I wanted, but was misplacing my trust in people and being hurt. So really I just wanted to get control of my life. I'd sorted out my career and my health. I'd started to get physically fit and I'd stopped smoking a few years before, so I asked myself, "Why can't I get control of my love life? Instead of waiting for somebody else, why don't I try this – it's been offered to me." You clearly weren't a rip-off, which is a danger with dating agencies. You didn't charge an excessive amount and it seemed to me, having run a small business myself, that what you were charging was a fair covering of your costs plus a little profit. That was important to me – a clear indication that you were genuine. When I got your brochure, I thought, "Well, this is somebody trying to do some good." There was no guarantee you were going to work magic, but there was no harm in trying. What is important about your agency is the fact that people who have joined it have come to you knowing what they want in life, and that's a huge step forward.'

Fraser knew he wanted a wife and family. He'd had a relationship with a South African the previous year that didn't work out. Being on an island is tricky, because a lot of the girls move off after school. So, unless you happen to find the right partner early on, it's difficult to meet somebody who is right. His father had been in the army: Fraser was born in Germany and lived there until the age of three, when the family moved to Hampshire and then to Aviemore in the Highlands before they ended up on the Isle of Skye when he was seven. His mother was the farmer in their family, and it was the same with Mary, which is quite a strange coincidence. And both parents had come to farming late in life compared to most people. So both Fraser and Mary had shared experiences, together with a general broadness of experience that was unusual in farming people.

Fraser told me, 'I suppose I'd been thinking all winter that I wasn't getting any younger and opportunities weren't exactly landing on my doorstep. One evening my mother threw the *Farmers' Weekly* at me, open at the page advertising your bureau – little did she know what she was starting. I suppose she wanted me to marry and come back to the farm and retain the lifestyle. As it turned out, she was disappointed with the outcome, not imagining a wife would have her own farm. I suppose I was quite sceptical about applying to an introduction agency but I thought I had nothing to lose – gets you out of the house, and why not? I was quite excited about the idea of meeting someone. I thought it would be tricky to find anyone remotely near, and I knew it was going to be difficult to meet because of the way farming is – you can't just disappear and go here, there and everywhere, and money was a consideration because I didn't have any! No, it was obviously going to be difficult for me. I needed to be sure that I wanted to meet a woman – that we had enough in common – before going to that effort.'

I spoke on the phone for some time to Mary, and the phrase that she kept repeating to me to describe her perfect match was 'an intelligent sheep farmer'. She also said she didn't mind where I lived because she had to travel from London anyway. Fraser too was open-minded about who he met, as long as he didn't have to waste time with women who would be totally unsuited to farming life on a remote island.

They both filled in their basic information forms, and Mary commented on how strange it was to find out about people via that small piece of prose. She said she was impressed by Fraser's admission that he played the accordion, and in brackets 'badly!'. If somebody could joke about himself like that, she thought, it sounded like fun. Fraser said that when he discovered Mary had been to university he decided she must have some brains, and the fact that she described herself as gentle, vivacious and possessing a good sense of humour definitely interested him. He added, though, that when she said her first love was sheep farming he felt this could be artistic licence.

They found out a lot about each other in the first letters. Mary was in an awkward situation where she was sharing a flat with a male friend, and, without making a big thing about it, she didn't want Fraser to think she was involved with him – her flatmate was gay. She emphasised that she was considering moving back to North Wales to her parents' farm at the end of the year. This move was for two reasons: she was fed up with London and she wanted to spend time with them. She loved her parents dearly, and regretted the long years she had been away from them in London. They were getting older and were a little unwell, so to move back was what she really wanted to do. She talked about her work. She had wanted to be an actress and had ended up being an agent for comedians such as Michael Bentine and Jon Pertwee. In fact the death of Willie Rushton, who was her friend and client, was a trigger for her. She described her last meeting with him.

'He was one of the best people to work with, and when he died I thought, "I've worked with the best now – I can't better that." Willie died undergoing routine heart surgery, and the last time I saw him he was hiding under his bed sheets at the hospital and he said, "Oh, the curse of Mary." I said, "Don't be so ridiculous! It's only heart surgery. We've still got shows to do." In fact he was laughing about the brochure you're given before the operation – it says that after recovery you can hang-glide and parachute and go rock climbing, and he said, "Marvellous, I've never been able to do those things before. I'm really looking forward to it." But he didn't pull through, and it really knocked me for six. And his death made me think, "Right, I've been messing about, thinking about moving. I'm going to set myself a year to leave, tidy up loose ends, sort my life out, get fit and go back to North Wales." It felt like home even though I hadn't grown up there. Spiritually, it felt like my home. And this was the same sort of time I was in touch with Fraser. Gradually things became clearer.'

Mary's letters were full of jokes and humour to cover her nervousness, whereas Fraser's were slightly more factual. He remembered getting out the silver letter opener to open Mary's first letter and thinking, 'Well, is this it? Is this the person I'll marry?' And Mary admitted to not knowing where the Isle of Skye was and having to look it up on a map. The song 'Over the Sea to Skye' kept going round in her head . . .

They both agreed that this had been an ideal way to get to know each other, and a very exciting part of their relationship. The postman played an important role in their early romance – to see the familiar handwriting and wonder what was inside (maybe another photo as well as a letter), and then to read the writer's thoughts, ponder on them, think of a reply, and then be able to put it somewhere safe and private and read it again and again, was a great pleasure. Letters can tell so much about a person – even the handwriting is very revealing.

I commented that Mary was living a very different lifestyle from Fraser's and asked him how he reacted. He said he thought it was interesting, and Mary admitted that her extrovert and unusual way of life had put other men off, so it was a good sign that Fraser wanted to carry on.

After three months of writing, they got round to speaking. One day Fraser's mother told him he was wanted on the phone, and he was very surprised to find it was Mary calling completely out of the blue. They found it delightful to talk to each other after all the letters, and couldn't wait for the phone calls. Mary recalls perching on the kitchen table in her poky London flat to talk. 'You know, I can picture it now. I would sit on the kitchen table in the flat, my feet dangling off, and talk for ages. And all I could think of was the life Fraser had and where he was phoning from, and the dogs barking and the cows, and longing for it. Really I'd started to push my own life away – the London life – and knew instinctively that I wanted this type of life, and down that phone line came a glimmer of it, and it was joyful, and we did make each other laugh. His calls just lit up my life.'

Fraser even considered getting a phone in his bedroom

(an unprecedented thought, as he was quite shy on the phone) since farmers generally go to bed early, and he didn't want to wake his parents. 'What struck me most,' he said, 'was her incredible sense of humour and her caring attitude. I thought, "You can get a long way in life with somebody who will laugh at most things." However bad things are, if you can have a joke about it it makes all the difference, and I thought there was certainly a possibility here.'

But then they realised that, although this was great, they were completely flummoxed by the practical problems of sustaining a relationship over such a distance. It was fine writing and it was lovely phoning, but how do you get to know somebody physically – would they find each other attractive?

Mary told me, 'We were really worried about the next step, which was having a meeting, and we had to think what would happen if we didn't click. I thought we would, knowing how well we were getting on, but he might think I was really ugly – and vice versa. The chemistry is so important – we have to accept that we have to be attracted to someone physically.' They found it very difficult to make the first move towards a meeting, both because of the physical distance and because of fear of disappointment. Both admitted that they were terrified of seeing each other for the first time. But they eventually decided that they would have a weekend together in Glasgow, which is roughly halfway time-wise between London and the Isle of Skye.

They had by now swapped photographs of each other.

Fraser had bravely sent one of himself in swimming trunks and another with his new tractor, while Mary had opted for one taken several years ago in flared trousers, updated by a more rustic and appropriate shot of herself with a sheep. So, with the letters and phone calls and photos, they did have some idea of what to expect, but their hopes and fears were running high that Saturday morning when the London train pulled into the station in Glasgow.

Mary told me she was very nervous – although she has the actor's ability to conceal her nerves and appear outwardly confident – while inwardly she was terrified. 'I wanted to look my most attractive, but in control. I wore a smart suit – trousers and a bright green blazer – I guess what I would have worn to meet an important client in London. I wanted to impress him. I had heels on – not very high.'

Fraser said he had never been so scared in his life. He was standing at the end of the platform. Lots of people had gone past, and it had got to the stage where there was only one door swinging in the wind and he still hadn't spotted her. He thought she hadn't come.

Mary explained. 'I'd got off the train and I saw this chap who looked very like the photograph – you can't always tell from a photograph – and I did my usual trick. If I'm not sure it's somebody, as I come level with them I say their name. So as I came level, I said "Fraser?" and there was no response at all. I didn't realise Mr Nervous had gone completely deaf. There was no response, so I thought, "Crikey, it's not him." How embarrassing is that? I was so nervous. I walked past him and put my suitcase down and just stood there looking at his back. And I saw these rather hunky, broad shoulders gradually start to fall and get lower, because he thought I wasn't on the train. And he turned round very forlornly to sort of slope off, and I just looked at him and said, "I think you're waiting for me." And that was it.'

Fraser's first response to Mary was to feel daunted by her clothes, which they both described as 'London'. He had his smart leather jacket on and was feeling very well dressed by Skye standards. Later he admitted he had found her manner rather cold, and she said that this was how she sometimes came across when she was trying to cover her nervousness with super-confidence.

Anyway, they somehow managed to get themselves off the station and into Fraser's car. He had carefully planned a weekend of sightseeing and had booked hotels for two nights, one in Glasgow, one in Fort William. Mary had complicated matters by trying to do business while she was in Glasgow. She had made arrangements to meet a new client, an up-and-coming comedian who lived there. Unfortunately he was good-looking and charming, and Fraser's jealousy was immediately aroused. In a way, with hindsight, this was probably not a bad thing. There's nothing like a bit of competition to spur a man into action!

They had a disastrous meal at an awful Chinese restaurant. Neither could eat anything, and Fraser's hands were literally shaking. Then they went to the cinema to see, most appropriately, *Mrs Brown* – the film about Queen Victoria and her Scottish manservant. They dropped their popcorn all over the floor. It had not been a very good start. Both said that, during those first few hours, they had kept looking at the other and thinking, 'Is this the person I'm going to marry?'

Mary told me, 'This was so different from a usual first date – there was so much subtext. But, because of the way we were introduced via your agency, we knew we were telling the truth, and that we both wanted to get married and have children. We knew that about each other before we met, and we'd had six months' preparation. This was very important and we both wanted it to be right, and it was very strange – just like one of those arranged marriages. This is what's so refreshing about your agency – knowing where somebody's coming from. No games, no messing about, nobody's lying.'

At the end of that first day together, they still hadn't touched and went to their separate beds, exhausted and wondering what would happen next. The next day they drove to Fort William. Mary described her feelings. 'We had to get to know each other, and it was too important to mess it up. The Scottish air hit me and I kept falling asleep in the car. I kept looking at Fraser in the driver's seat and wondering, "Can I spend my life with this man?" There were tiny little white blobs on his ears (I can't even see them now), and I thought, "There's no way I can spend the rest of my life with this man." I thought his face was too small. Of course it isn't, but I got fixated with this. I kept wondering what he thought of me.' But they had a good time wandering around the hills and lochs of Glencoe, gently flirting and getting to know one another.

They spent that night in an awful hotel. Fraser had booked a double room. Mary described how, before their meal, they were getting ready together in the same room. Fraser was cleaning his shoes, which had got muddy from their walking during the day. Mary was sitting at the dressing table putting her earrings on, and she remembered quite clearly thinking, 'Am I going to be doing things like this for the rest of my life, with this man?' Yet, she had to admit to herself, it didn't feel too uncomfortable. 'Here was a man I'd met twenty-four hours ago, and we were about to go to supper – we'd not touched really, and yet this felt so right.'

The meal was not a huge success, but afterwards they went up to their room, consumed a good deal of malt whisky (described by Mary as the shy person's friend) and gradually came to share their first kiss and their first night together as lovers. Jane Austen would have finished her story shortly after the first kiss, I suppose, but for Fraser and Mary there were many more tests.

Having discovered that they were probably falling in love, they now had to go back to their real lives 500 miles apart. Fraser told me how incredibly painful it was saying goodbye, and of course they had to do this many times before they finally lived together. He said that the person doing the travelling has an easier time than the person left behind, because the traveller can concentrate on the journey whereas the one left behind can only mooch around and think of the loss and the loved one getting further and further away.

After their first meeting, Mary finalised her plans to move back to the family farm in Snowdonia. Her mother was ill and not going to recover. Fraser made the journey to Wales, and was initiated into the family by being asked to trim the pigs' trotters! It was pouring with rain, Fraser recalled – not unusual, of course, in Wales, and something he would eventually have to get used to. Mary also made the journey to the Isle of Skye, and loved the place. She commented on the number of very attractive men there, and lamented the fact that they would probably never get the chance to meet a partner.

After a year or so of going back and forth they were both feeling frustrated by being so far apart, but while Fraser was ready to make a move Mary was having doubts. Fraser went to Wales, wanting to propose, but when Mary met him off the train he said he could sense her apathy – he said it was sort of, 'Oh, you're here, then', not joyful at all.

Mary recalled some of the details. 'Fraser wanted to get me out of the house, somewhere romantic. He wanted to go for a walk. And I was worried about what he wanted to do. I didn't know if he was going to propose, and I wanted to put it off. I was rejecting the relationship a bit at that time because I was scared it was getting too serious. I was in a very strange mood – probably hormonal. Getting me out of the house was like getting a limpet off a rock. Eventually he got me out and we went to feed the sheep. We'd gone through the gate, in our waterproofs, mud-soaked. I stood there dripping, and he got down on one knee and proposed up on the mountainside – it was so lovely. And I did say yes, although I was confused.'

She asked Fraser not to tell anybody. This was her reason: 'I had this conflict, common to my generation of women, about commitment and career, and is this the right person, and being scared. I said yes, but my mind was whirling. The trouble is, we're all fed a diet of knights in shining armour, whereas what I had in reality was this decent, good-looking, nice man who I was terribly comfortable with, but wasn't fireworks and parties every night and travelling round the world. Maybe the knight in shining armour was round the next corner. But the guy who produces the fireworks is not the guy you want to spend your life with. The comfortable alternative sometimes puts people off because lots of us want to live on the edge. What I've learnt now is that companionship, trust and laughter are so important, and it can seem fuddy duddy – but it's not, it's real. And we do have our firework moments.'

I get a lot of this sort of attitude from women (and men) in their thirties and forties. They find it almost impossible to make a commitment in case something better turns up along the line. I don't really know what the answer is here, but in my experience, for marriage or a long-term relationship to work, in almost every case there has to be give and take, compromise and a willingness to take the long view.

But at this point fate put on her gumboots and waded

right in. Exuberant celebrations (Dutch courage maybe?) led to Mary becoming pregnant. But, far from this being a disaster for her, it put everything in perspective, and she was absolutely certain that marriage was right. For her this was a message, saying 'This is the man for you.' Without that, she admitted that she would probably still be trying to make up her mind.

Mary didn't want to tell Fraser over the phone, and she didn't want to tell her parents before Fraser, so she had a terrible time. In Wales they were going through lambing, which is very dangerous for pregnant women as they can pick up a virus from contact with the lamb foetus. If it gets into the woman's bloodstream it can have very adverse consequences on the unborn child. She was putting on gloves to deliver lambs, and her parents thought she was behaving a bit strangely.

They met up again in Glasgow and went out for dinner, over which Mary broke the news. Fraser was very surprised – it was, amazingly, something he hadn't considered. But of course, like Mary, he felt it made the decision to marry so much easier. I was amused at this statement, 'something he hadn't considered', and smiled at the power of human nature. Here were two intelligent human beings who had travelled considerably and been successful in their lives; who certainly witnessed the facts of life every day and had possibly made mature decisions on how to conduct their love life. But against all that, old human nature comes along and does what she has been doing for centuries – informs us that we are not going to get the better of her and she will show us who is boss, and Mary became pregnant.

Mary described the next few months as like 'staggering through fog'. She said, 'We kept seeing problems that seemed insurmountable, and then, when it was right, the fog cleared and we could see how to take the next step. We had two farms, both of which were great to work. Fraser's parents wanted us to farm there, and my parents wanted us to farm here. But my mother was dying, we knew, so that was a trauma to get through. We had all these problems, with my mum's illness and having the baby, and we were constantly worried about how we would actually settle down and have a life together. We knew we would be upsetting one party or another wherever we decided to farm.'

All their wedding preparations were made long-distance. They had to meet up to choose a wedding ring. Mary's mother did a lot of the organising. Mary said, 'I found that I was able to relax and not think it was anything to do with me, and I think it's a good bit of advice for brides with mothers like mine. Fraser and I quite fancied a nice quiet Quaker wedding because that's my faith, and Fraser's quite shy. It would have quite suited us, but Mum wouldn't have that. Then it dawned on us that what she was planning was her own farewell party. And as it turned out it was the right thing and the best party ever. It was a brilliant day. Her present to us was the fireworks at the end of the wedding. The whole mountainside was lit up: it was spectacular, a glorious send-off, a celebration of her life and our marriage. Fraser's father very kindly paid for our honeymoon as a wedding present. I remember watching the sunset on the rocks at Ibiza. We knew we had a very bumpy time ahead of us, with my mum's health, the dilemma of where we were going to farm, a child on the way – only three months left of just the two of us. So we were in the extraordinary circumstance of having spent so little time together as a couple without children. But we knew we could share it together. The vicar at the wedding asked everybody to rally round us because of the rough ride ahead. And people have – they've been fantastic. Everybody loves the story of how we got together, and it inspires people.'

Instead of Fraser and Mary returning to the Isle of Skye after their honeymoon, they decided to go to live in Wales. It was quite difficult for his mother because he had said they would go back to Skye once things had resolved in Wales. But they didn't know how long that would be, so decisions had to be made about getting a permanent farm worker to replace Fraser or to get somebody who'd help part-time. What actually happened was that the person in the farm bungalow said he would do the feeding, and so they left it at that.

Fraser and Mary rented a small house close to the farm in Snowdonia, and very much enjoyed being alone together for the first time. Three months later, a daughter was born – very quickly, on the living room floor. They didn't even come close to putting all their detailed plans for a water birth at the local hospital into effect. As it turned out, the postman alerted everyone and within half an hour their first-born came into the world, with Mary lying on newspapers, which had quickly been spread all over the floor, and half the village in attendance! The baby was a joy to them all, especially Mary's mother who by then was spending most of her days in bed. She was able to nurse the baby for many hours and developed a lovely and very special rapport with her new little grand-daughter, knowing full well that she wouldn't live to see her grow up.

As time went by it became more and more urgent to make some serious decisions, primarily about where they would live. 'We both saw the problems,' Mary told me, 'but Fraser just had faith that they would resolve. There's an expression that what's for you won't go by you. He kept quoting it to me, and I asked what he meant, but he was right in the end.'

Fraser's very wise comment was: 'It's hard to take too many bridges at once – you can't do it. You're looking at a great stack of bridges, and you think you can't do it. But if you take them one at a time you can.' 'And I thought he was right and that we could do it, but one at a time,' added Mary. 'And what's so nice is that we're crossing those bridges together now, and all sorts of other problems come up in our lives, but it's so nice to have a partner to walk side by side with across that bridge. It makes it a lot easier.'

Mary's mother died a few months after the arrival of their new daughter. She was a woman of great energy, strength and wisdom for her family and had a high reputation in the farming community of Wales. For Mary, and for Fraser who had grown to love her dearly, it was hard to let her go, to keep her all-consuming memory with them but let her now rest, without pain and in peace. But with time they learnt to do so.

They felt that in order to make a decision on where to farm they would need to spend time in both places. But then Mary fell pregnant again and they decided to stay in Wales for the birth.

Fraser went up with a van containing all their belongings. It's about a ten-hour drive without stops, then a ferry, then another hour's driving. So it's a full day door to door. On the way back the van broke down at three o'clock in the morning. The four of them moved into a bungalow on the farm in Skye and joined in the local life. And then, in spite of being on the pill, Mary fell pregnant again. The local doctor, hearing her history, commented in good dry Scottish fashion, 'My, we are fertile, aren't we?'

They faced a dilemma, but they also felt they were very lucky, with two beautiful farms to choose from. In the end they chose to live in Snowdonia for practical reasons. Fraser said, 'Probably the crux was the long-term financial prognosis. Farming is going through such bad times, and to farm on an island is doubly hard because everything you bring in you pay for – probably about £300 to bring a lorry-load of hay over on the ferry. You have to take your stock off to market. The buyers know you're from an island and you won't want to be taking them back, so you get rock-bottom prices.' Mary added, 'And because this is Snowdonia it's attracting environmental schemes. There's more potential here. We really had to make the decision on those grounds. And for children, the opportunities on the island were fewer. People do survive there very well, but we had a choice.'

So the lonely farmer from a remote Scottish island and the actress from London had a happy ending (although nothing ever really ends). While I was talking to them the children kept wanting attention, there was farm work waiting, dinner to get ready and a hundred other things to do. But for one moment I saw Mary standing by the Aga with the baby in her arms and the other two at her feet, and I knew it was the image of contentment she had always wanted.

7
The North Wind
Doth Blow . . .

I don't want pig farmers to feel I put them all in the same category as the one I had to chastise for smelling absolutely awful. Far from it. I think that the great majority of farmers, and particularly pig farmers, turn out to be exceedingly presentable and virtually smelling of roses when they go out. I certainly remember one pig farmer, Jeremy, as being one of the sweetest-smelling, nicest people I've ever met. An absolutely sincere man with no pretensions, he had a few flaws (don't we all?) but they weren't great and he was quite honest about them.

He came to the bureau for an interview one day in late September. His marriage had ended after about twenty years – mostly, I think, due to his lifestyle. After being by himself for a number of years he had got into a muddle with the farm paperwork and the house. He was an intelligent, cultured man and, as well as being a farmer, he was a boy scout leader, a role which he enjoyed very much. He was determined, no matter what the workload was at the farm or how difficult the rest of his life had become, to carry on with this, as it was his one escape from the day-to-day grind of farm work.

He sat down in one of my big comfortable chairs and said, 'I'm going to ask you to do the impossible.'

'Go ahead,' I said. 'I love a challenge.'

'Well, I'd like you to find my dream woman. I'd like her to be around my age, petite in build, and to be able to help me with my paperwork. It would be so good if she knew about pig farming and could help out with that as well. And someone who would get my house tidy and presentable again. Oh – and not living too far away. I just haven't got the time to travel a great distance to see someone. And I would love to meet someone who would understand my enjoyment of the scouts.'

'Yes, that's all quite challenging,' I said, taking a deep breath. 'Very challenging, in fact.' We went on talking and then I started looking through my register. I was by myself in the admin room of the office, having left Jeremy in the interview room drinking coffee.

There and then, looking through my register, I found Ellie and wondered if she could be the woman for him. She lived about eight miles from him, and as I kept reading things got better. She was a farm secretary and a farmer's daughter, she had described how her father mostly kept pigs, and last but by no means least she was a girl guide leader! I just about fell off the office chair – they're not very stable at the best of times, are they? I couldn't believe it. This last attribute actually stopped me in my tracks; I thought he must know her, being so close and connected with the guides.

When I started to tell Jeremy about Ellie his eyes lit up

and he exclaimed, over and over again, 'No, I don't know her. I don't, really I don't.'

That afternoon a very satisfied Jeremy left my office. As he left, he had to walk round a huge heap of straw that had been delivered in the previous hour or two. Several trailer loads had been deposited, but as it was after milking and the men had gone home John had the whole lot to stack by himself. Jeremy started talking to him, and without any hesitation said he was going to stop and help stack it all away. It was an incredibly kind gesture, and they both worked well into the evening.

The most marked thing about autumn with us is that we have loads and loads of straw delivered, usually at the most inconvenient moments. But it is all essential to be stacked away for animal bedding through the winter. I don't think any livestock farmer enjoys autumn, for he or she is continually thinking that winter, with all the work that it brings, is just around the corner. However, no one can deny the splendour of this season, especially when the low sun twinkles through the trees that surround our farm, highlighting all the tones of green, rust and gold. Our trees grow in a horseshoe shape around the house and buildings, obviously planted deliberately many years ago to shelter us from the north. Then, radiating away across the fields, are other woods curving around in an arc that acts as a windbreak. Having many acres of woodland we are able to keep ourselves going in logs throughout the winter, but it takes about two to three weeks' continual sawing of the fallen trees to stack enough wood to see us through.

I'm sure some people visualise me at this time of year as a typical farmer's wife, continually picking and freezing and jamming soft fruit. I used to, but I was never so pleased as when one year some young stock blustered their way into the orchard and trampled down those damned blackcurrant bushes, which I'm pleased to say have never recovered. I would far rather be matchmaking than jam-making.

In the course of time Jeremy and Ellie were introduced, and it turned out that her father had just retired from pig farming and was at his wit's end to find something to do. As time went by I was told that, as Ellie's father got to know Jeremy through his daughter, he started coming round to the farm most days to give Jeremy a hand. It certainly both helped Jeremy and gave Ellie's father something to do in his retirement. And of course she put his paperwork right with her farm secretarial expertise.

The next phone call I got was from Ellie herself. She told me that Jeremy's house was really not as bad as he'd made out. 'In fact, once I'd cleaned up the smelly socks and dust I actually discovered it was really beautiful.' About six months afterwards, Jeremy phoned and asked if he and Ellie could call in to see me. When they turned up about a week afterwards they announced with beaming smiles and hugging each other that they had had a quiet registry office wedding and this was the third day of their honeymoon. Ellie's father had moved into the farmhouse for a week to look after the farm. They were in a dreamlike state of deep happiness – possibly the most perfectly matched pig farmers in the world!

Of course, it doesn't go right every time. A few weeks later another farmer came for an interview. A vegetable merchant with a small farm, he actually brought me a gift of several sacks of potatoes and an assortment of vegetables. He explained he was on his way to deliver a consignment of vegetables to a new customer, and I presumed that was why he had turned up in his large commercial van. He was a straightforward man who after a few weeks received his first introduction, but I got a surprise when the lady in question telephoned me the day after their first date and said she didn't want to see him again. I'm always a little apprehensive when I hear these words – what awful things have happened?

'He arrived in his big vegetable van,' she complained, 'and when I climbed inside the only place for me to sit was on a sack of potatoes where the passenger seat should have been! I was supposed to bounce happily all evening on this bag of potatoes as he drove round doing his deliveries!'

Thinking of potatoes always reminds me of bonfire night when the children were small. The men would build a mound of wood and rubbish all week. In the evening many of the children's friends and their parents came along, and we all sat around the fire on straw bales watching the fireworks at the bottom of the field. I lit a smaller fire on which I cooked all the food. A parent brought a guitar and serenaded us as we toasted our feet and faces, and then we all turned round to warm our backs as well.

Tupping always takes place around bonfire night on

our farm. This is when we put the ram with the ewes, so that they can go forth and multiply the following spring. One late autumn day Richard and Charlie, our two farm workers (a classic duo of the experienced teaching the inexperienced), put the ram in with his new harem. Wow! he thought all his Christmases had come at once. There was no thought of foreplay – instant action was on the agenda, and in the course of about ten minutes he mounted one sheep after the other. Charlie had stopped to light his baccy, and he and Richard were leaning on the gate and taking in the action. Then, without any warning, the stud of the day fell down dead! Charlie took in the scene and turned slowly to Richard, who was standing open-mouthed. 'Now let that that be a lesson to thee, lad. Pace thyself – if thou does the same thing as yon ram, thou'll end up dead as well.'

As we come closer to Christmas the bureau office gets busier. Sadly, people realise they will be alone over this holiday time and seem desperate to find a partner quickly. They remember seeing other couples having a good time together and cannot stand the thought of being left out for yet another year. The Christmas season seems to emphasise the family bliss that we are all supposed to enjoy, and when you are not in that situation but want it so much your whole life seems completely empty. I know of one North Wales farmer who at Christmas always leaves the farm for his married brother to look after and goes abroad on holiday – just so he doesn't have to face the continual sorrow of being alone.

About two weeks before Christmas I stop sending

letters out and constantly telephone people – it concludes introductions more quickly. I would never want anyone to be waiting over the holiday period for the information they need to get in touch with a suitable partner. The evening of the last working day before the bureau office breaks for Christmas has always been the time for my secretaries and me to have a good 'girlie' night out together. We'll have a long lingering meal out and reminisce over the work we've completed that year, with the humour that all offices experience when dealing with people. Secretaries who have left a few years previously are also invited and ask about remembered clients. Sometimes we invite the farm staff and the bureau staff to join together, and that's always a hilarious evening of jibes and taunting and jokes.

Christmas Day on the farm isn't really much different from any other day. The milking and feeding still have to be done, but we always try to make sure everything is finished as early as possible on Christmas morning. Usually all the men have these holiday days off except Harold, who will beg to come in on Christmas Day to milk. He has a large and close family living nearby but says he couldn't stand sitting in the house all day having nothing to do. Harold is a tall, thin man who never says a lot. When he does, it's sensible and to the point, but you could go for days without having a conversation with him. We've never been sure how old he is, but he has worked for us for twenty-two years with scarcely a day's sickness. All his sons have worked for us too, either full-time or casually over the years, and we have gone through our family difficulties with him and his wife; they were always there for us when we had troubled times. You could set your watch by him, for if you see Harold getting the cows in or performing some other task you would know the exact time as he never varies for even a minute.

Charlie has worked for us longer than anyone full-time. He stands about six foot three, with a closely cut beard, and seems larger than life. He's no fool, and is actually the wittiest person I know: faced with any situation, he can always come up with remarks to make you rock with laughter. My secretary Lynda, the good-looking one, was on the phone when the farm was struck by lightning. She received quite a shock and went running over to the men's room for safety and a cup of tea to steady her nerves. Charlie told us next day, 'I adopted the two principles of first aid. I made her lie on the floor and loosened her clothing.' 'That was a bit of wishful thinking if ever I heard it!' she said the next day.

He's the first to admit he's not over-clever, and from time to time reminds us all that 'without thick buggers like me shovelling shit, the world would come to a stop'. Of course he's right. We can't all be university graduates, and we will always need good basic practical men like our Charlie.

He formed part of the best duo we ever had on the farm when young Richard was also working for us. There was an age gap of about twenty years between them, but they bounced off each other verbally with a fantastically funny repertoire. A few minutes in their company and you would be in fits of laughter. Richard is a big, broad lad, about six foot two with a round, ruddy face. He says himself that he is not a walking encyclopaedia, but he has a heart of gold and you could trust him with your life.

One morning he talked at length to Charlie about a complaint he had, and thought maybe he should go and see the doctor.

'Oh, you've got gonorrhoea, mate,' Charlie said to him.

'What's that?' asked the bewildered Richard.

'It's best to go and tell Pat what's wrong. Tell her about it and she'll have a look at you and put you right.'

Richard promptly came to me in the house and said he needed some advice. As he sat down at the kitchen table he announced, 'I've got gonorrhoea.'

I immediately thought that this was a first, and went into my 'nothing can surprise me' mode! But after a few moments I blurted out, 'I'm so sorry, Richard. How do you know?'

'It's painful,' he said. 'Will you have a look at it?'

I knew I was the elected first aider for the farm and a nurse to boot, but this was beyond the call of duty. 'I don't think so,' I said. 'Best see your doctor.'

'If you say so,' he said. 'But I'll have to have time off work, and I thought you could just have a look at it down there and see what you think.'

'God! What am I going to do now?' I thought.

Then at that moment he angled his ear up against my face. 'Down there,' he said. 'Just look down my ear. I think I've got some wax in it.'

Only then did I fully comprehend, and twigged the mischief Charlie had been up to. 'Who mentioned gonorrhoea to you, Richard?' I asked.

'Charlie. He said I'd got it in my ear.'

Richard could be a little bit hapless as well as gullible, and there was one particular incident when he got on the wrong side of our slurry tanker which really sticks in the memory. In the winter a livestock farmer usually likes a mild frost to harden the earth so he can spread his muck easier, without the continual tractor work damaging his ground. Yes, livestock farming still consists of muck, slurry and smell. Many days are taken up scurrying around spreading the stuff here, there and everywhere. One day Richard was doing this task with our slurry tanker. Slurry is the vile-smelling raw runny manure collected directly from the cubicle sheds where the dairy herd are housed in the winter. As with so many things that Richard touched, it all went wrong and a 'blowback' occurred. He stood in the yard with every square inch of him from head to foot covered in this foul-smelling excrement, dripping in large blobs over the ground. He looked just like the monster from the deep as he stood there, only his white teeth contrasting with the huge mass of brown muck.

At the end of January a few years ago there was such a bad frost that there was hardly any time left in the day after thawing out all the water pipes for the routine jobs of milking, mucking out and feeding, let alone spreading muck. Once we'd done everything the pipes froze again, so, as with painting the Forth Bridge, we were constantly going back to the beginning to start again.

At over 1000 feet above sea level it would be a miracle to get through a winter without snow, and the snow may well bring long days of back-breaking hard work. Other people, those in the lowlands and non-farmers, might look on snowfall with glee and anticipation. The Christmas card image fills their minds. But for the livestock farmer it's a very different picture.

The last week of January starts to give a glimmer of hope. The days are lengthening, and sometimes the snowdrops at the end of our drive start to show and this fills us with anticipation of the spring to come. The men say, 'Snowdrops are out – it'll soon be spring', but we all know that we're trying to deceive ourselves. On such a day in late January a few years ago, exclamations of 'Did you see the snowdrops?' came from all and sundry. But by ten o'clock that morning fluffy little snowflakes had started to drift across our view. 'How pretty they look,' I thought, but of course I wouldn't have dared utter such sentimental rubbish to John, who would have told me forcefully where to stick such daftness.

By eleven 'o'clock it was settling and the air was thick with the snowflakes that were now not so fluffy but downright large and thick, turning the whole skyline into a white haze. Without any warning the wind got up, and when you ventured no further than the farmyard little whirlwinds of blinding snow wrapped around you. As the men struggled around the corners of the buildings great sheets of windy snow would envelop them. I retreated to the house with my full buckets of coal and baskets of wood just as John appeared with the three workmen.

'We're going to get those heifers up from the fields – if we can get 'em to walk down through all this.' The men came in to put on coats and gloves – you never know with the stubbornness and cussedness of animals how long things will take.

I couldn't take my eyes from the windows. How quickly it seemed to be settling! I made a decision about what had been really bothering me – yes, I would go and fetch the children from school because, at this rate, if I left it for another hour or two the school bus wouldn't be able to get up to the village. I phoned the school and they seemed quite surprised. 'Well, there isn't much snow here in Bakewell, Mrs Warren – just a few flakes.' I explained that we were many hundreds of feet higher then them, but only after absolute insistence on my part was I reluctantly believed and a promise was made that the children would be waiting for me.

For women who are not too happy about driving in snow, thank God for 4 × 4 vehicles. The Toyota pick-up is the best to use, and I set off on the most direct route to the school. The roads were thickly covered with snow by this time, so I had to be very cautious because for several days there had been severe frost and they were now extremely icy. My dread is driving downhill and losing control of the vehicle – I know I'm a wimp on these occasions. I have to drive down a steep valley and across the river. Yet it's so beautiful when it's transformed into a magical winter landscape with a pheasant or two jumping out on to the stone bridge that it could easily win any Christmas card competition.

The children were astounded to have received an SOS message to wait in the bus bay for their mother to pick them up, and gleeful at having such an unexpected half-holiday. I drove back through the village and stopped to get some bread. Of course the children decided that emergency rations definitely included sweets. As we drove out of the village towards the long, steep hill I decided to get as much momentum as possible and therefore drove through the village at the highest speed I dared use. About a third of the way up I came across a car that was sliding back down. I'm afraid I passed it and felt a little guilty, but I knew that by sliding back down it would eventually come into the village and be fine.

At last we were home. I couldn't see the farm, how-ever, because by now the whole landscape had become a whiteout and, with the wind and heaviness of falling snow, we could only see a short distance in front of us. Once we were inside the house I made the fire up, mopped up the snow falling from our coats and shoes and thought of the meal I must get. Normally it would be something really gut-hugging and hot in this weather, but I didn't have enough time. John and the men who had been out to collect the heifers were at the door and crowding into the utility room. 'We can't get the buggers to turn down and walk into the wind, heading down into the buildings. We've tried everything.' And as he said this I could see they were like three snowmen – absolutely covered! 'We're going to take some food up to them after dinner and see what we can do when this wind dies down. We've got to start thinking about what happens if the milk tanker can't get to us, too.'

Soaking wet gloves and caps were put on and around the Rayburn to dry as quickly as possible and the melting snow dripped into puddles on the floor and on to the cat sitting by the Rayburn. The cat and I do not get on. We have an ongoing dislike of each other; she knows it and I know it, but when John sits down she immediately goes and sits on his lap and looks at me as if she's saying, 'I'm on his lap and you aren't – he prefers me to you.'

I quickly got together soup, bread and cheese. The kids complained because they had missed their great school dinners. 'I was going to have Chow Mein today,' Ben announced, and Sarah protested that her favourite prawn cocktail lunch was not on the farmhouse menu. 'Tough luck!' I exclaimed, or similar words to express the fact that I didn't feel much sympathy for their situation.

The wind continued to howl and the snow was falling even faster, so we decided to telephone around to see where the milk tanker had got to. It was located between ourselves and Ashbourne, where it had become bogged down on a farm drive and couldn't move. Colin, who was the driver and had collected our milk for seventeen years, was the most dedicated of men. He would move heaven and earth to get through to a farm, whatever the weather. But obviously these conditions had got the better even of him.

This is the most worrying thing about dairy farming. If you can't get your milk away you don't get paid for it and all your work literally goes down the drain. John and I and the men talked about what was to be done. 'We can pump the milk out of the normal tank into the emergency tank, so there's enough space for the milking this afternoon,' said John, as he directed one man to go and take fodder to the heifers up in the fields, another to bring the emergency tank to the dairy door, while he himself went to find and sort out the required pump. Ben volunteered to go up the fields with Charlie. Sarah wanted to build a snowman, and I was told I'd be needed outside soon.

I made up the fire again, went and fetched more coal and wood, considered what to get them for the next meal and also thought about the possibility of the men not going home that night. Then John put his head around the door with a great blast of cold air and said I'd got to go and stand outside and hold the pump by the emergency tank to make sure the milk was transferred without too much spillage. Harold and Richard were sent to start the routine jobs that were usually finished about midday.

The wind got even worse as I stood by the tank. I couldn't believe how bad it was, and yet I was standing in the sheltered farmyard. Whatever was it like on the exposed hillside? My fingers were numb, my eyes stinging from the constant battering of snowflakes. I dreamt as I stood there that my toes were in front of my lovely roaring fire and I was getting hotter and hotter. At last, after standing and holding the pump about a foot in the air for an hour, the transfer was over and we had an empty milk tank. The milking could then start – a little later than usual, but how lucky that this had gone so well. Harold would get the cows out of the cubicle shed; they had to come into the collecting yard adjacent to the shed and then walk into the milking parlour. It was only a few yards, but with the biting wind heading straight at them they would not be keen even to come out of their housing.

Back in the farmhouse I thought about the hot meal for later. I was sure there would be three extra men – seven of us in total. A stew, I thought, but there wasn't enough time to tenderise stewing steak or shin of beef. It would have to be a casserole using some better beef. Quickly I got the ingredients together and then decided to make an enormous rice pudding. I put all this in the oven, and after about half an hour the next surprise occurred.

The electricity went off. Was it me? No, I hadn't done anything. By that time of day it was dark, so I floundered for matches and candles. Noises came from the back door. 'Phone to see if it's the mains or us,' John shouted through to me. On outlying farms it's quite common for the electricity to go off and I know the telephone number by heart. 'Yes, quite a lot of your area are without electricity,' came the reply.

John's decision was that it would be best to put on our own generator and get the cows milked. When the generator is being used for milking we can't use it for anything in the house except for one or two lights. 'At least the meal will still cook with the retained heat of the Rayburn,' I thought.

Suddenly there was a knock on the door and I stood

there in shock, as I knew no ordinary vehicle could get up our drive. For a few seconds I wondered who on earth it could be. On opening the back door I saw a figure like the abominable snowman, breathless and trembling, covered from head to foot in snow and obviously freezing to death. It was Colin, our milk tanker driver. He walked in and started to tell me that he had managed to get from his Ashbourne collections to our area but hadn't been able to get his vehicle up the hill to us. So he'd decided to walk up to our farm to ask John to take the tractor down to his milk tanker and pull him up.

'Never mind that,' I said. 'Have you had anything to eat all day?'

He admitted that he hadn't and that he was starving.

'Well, you aren't doing anything until I've cooked you something,' I announced. Knowing that the Rayburn would still have some heat I set to and quickly cooked bacon, sausage, eggs and fried bread which Colin set about, all washed down by tea.

With his clothes warmed and food and drink inside him he seemed a different man. Colin always had a friendly word with me most mornings when he came on to the farm, but never chatted too long or gossiped about others. Determined as ever, he went outside to arrange with John the help he needed. I heard a tractor set off, and after a while the tanker trundled into the yard. Once again, in the midst of whirling snowflakes, the milk was transferred from the tanks. Our tractor pulled it down the drive and continued escorting it for a few miles until it got on to the main roads and was able slowly but steadily to get the milk back to the depot. Thank God for men like Colin – salt of the earth, with a highly committed and dependable spirit.

After what seemed an interminable length of time all the men came into the house, once again like snowmen, and unwrapped all their outer clothes. 'Well, I can't see any of you going home tonight,' said John. 'The thing is, if you went home there's the biggest chance that if it continues to snow like this you'd not get here tomorrow – and I shall need you more than ever tomorrow.'

There was a fair bit of muttering before the men agreed that John was right. The meal was eaten by the flickering light of candles, and then we discussed the sleeping arrangements. Although we have a guest bedroom, with no electricity we couldn't heat it. So it was decided they would all sleep in the sitting room with a settee each – thank goodness for our big farmhouse rooms, large enough to hold three comfy sofas – and toast themselves in front of the fire.

At first light next day it looked as if it hadn't snowed much more and the storm had blown itself out. What a relief! The men still had to do all the usual tasks on the snowbound farm, but I had made arrangements to visit some clients who had now married, Pauline and Jim, in Lancashire, so maybe I could still go. Their farm was in the lowlands, not so many miles away but light years in terms of winter weather.

8

A Nice Guy

The first part of my journey to Lancashire was quite difficult. There were no other vehicles on the hilltops – just oceans of snow. It actually got worse for a few miles as I negotiated the hazardous road leading past the Cat and Fiddle, the highest pub in England, but as I descended into the Cheshire plain the snow disappeared. And by the time I'd got into Lancashire the sun was shining and there was no evidence that back in Derbyshire we were in the depths of winter!

At Pauline and Jim's farm I was greeted with a hug from both and exclamations of 'Why have you driven all this way in the 4 × 4?' When I explained about the snow Jim said they had had some lovely sunny days – indeed, he'd been playing golf the day before. I thought they both looked at me as if I had dreamt it all up, but Pauline reassured me that she knew how different it was up in my part of the world. 'Remember, I lived high up for ten years,' she said.

I was taken into the long brick farmhouse, originally the farm buildings. They had retained some of the centuries-old features such as the large double doors for horse-drawn wagons, which was now a huge window spanning two floors. The two of them looked quite alike. One was tall and masculine and one was short and feminine, of course, but they both had friendly, ruddy, rural faces and blond hair, and both were slim in build and in their forties.

I asked Jim what had first attracted him to Pauline, and he said straightaway without having to think, 'Well, I'd really always thought that I would speak to anyone you asked me to, no matter what I thought of their profile. When I did talk to her for the first time I was quite impressed at how normal she seemed.' Pauline, in turn, said that when she read Jim's profile she was quite pleased that he had interests other than farming. I remembered her saying to me in her first week as a bureau member, 'I've got life in me, and I want to meet someone with a bit of life as well.' She went on to admit that she had always loved farm life but never wanted to exclude the possibility of a life outside farming.

Jim asked her to meet him and Pauline explained that her philosophy has always been that, if you spend a day with someone, even if you don't click you can have a nice day out and part as friends at the end of it. You haven't got to think, 'This could be the one', but take it as a day out with a friend.

On the way to Harrogate, where they had decided to meet, a most astonishing and traumatic thing happened to Jim. His ex-girlfriend sent him a message on his mobile phone at about 10 a.m. to tell him that he was now the father of a daughter born to her at 6.15 that morning.

He'd been in a relationship with this woman – not through the Farmers and Country Bureau – for about six months and it had broken off about eight months previously. The big thing was that he had never had children before – so what a shock it must have been for him, as he didn't even know she was pregnant! Pauline said, 'It must have been so difficult for him to continue his journey, and meet me, without showing his emotions.' Jim explained that he had had to stop the car for a few minutes to contemplate the news. 'My immediate thought was, "How do I know this child is mine?" My head was really full of it, swirling around. Then I thought about Pauline and knew she would be waiting, so I drove on.'

At Harrogate Jim kissed her on the cheek and immediately gave her a hug, which she thought that was a lovely warm gesture. They decided to go and have a meal, and Pauline left her car parked while they drove in his to the restaurant. When she got in his car the first thing she noticed was how similar their CD collections were. She sat there and said, 'Oh, I've got that . . . and I've got that too.' Spotting common ground continued with their talk over the lunch table. They liked eating the same things – ice cream, cream cakes, all the things you shouldn't eat. Jim added, 'I was determined not to meet someone who was paranoid about her weight and was constantly on a diet.' The day ended with another kiss – a bit more lingering this time.

On the way home Pauline told herself that this one was different. She said, 'He felt so comfortable – a warm and affectionate person, which I found so lovely and reassuring and something which I had been missing.'

They waited a fortnight before Jim visited Pauline's home. She lived in a cottage in the middle of nowhere up on the Pennines. 'Back of beyond,' Jim called it. 'A lovely spot but so exposed – so very, very different from where I live.' He explained how he had wanted to visit her home, for seeing how she kept it was very important to him. He admitted he could never be with someone who didn't like a nice clean house. 'Well, we both like a nice home,' Pauline added. What struck Jim when he met her again was that she was just the same as the first time. 'She hadn't changed,' he said. 'So often, over the years, I had met ladies who were false to begin with and changed as time went on – Pauline seemed totally unlike this.'

They admitted that on meeting this time an even more passionate kiss was exchanged. 'Very nice,' Jim said on reflection. They went for a walk, hand in hand, and decided the only way they would get to know each other was to keep talking and say what they thought and be truthful with each other. Jim said, 'What made the day for me was that when we came back after the walk she cooked me a meal, and I thought, "Thank goodness she likes her food and is willing to cook."'

They then went to meet Pauline's sister. She had apparently said how 'nice' Jim seemed to be, which he now cringed at and said, 'I hate the word "nice" when applied to men. That word conjures up quite a boring guy.'

'No, no,' Pauline and I protested. 'It means you're generally a lovely person.'

'But doesn't it mean you're boring? You see, I feel girls don't go for the ordinary, steadfast, salt-of-the-earth men – they usually go for someone who stands out of the crowd, not the nice guy.'

'Well, look what they're missing,' cried Pauline. 'I know what I perfer!'

I asked Jim to remind me about when he first contacted me, and he said he got in touch in 1983. He was introduced to several ladies and went out with one for several months, but then he met a local lady whom he eventually married. That marriage, he later realised, was never right because he felt he was on the rebound. They were actually married for twelve years but had no children. He then had a short relationship with the woman who had just had his child. Then he decided to come back to the bureau. 'I couldn't believe how you remembered me from fifteen years previously, but you did.'

Pauline said, 'I was fed up with meeting the wrong kind of men. I always read *Farmers' Weekly* and saw your ad week after week. I knew it was the agency that I wanted to join but I thought it was a lot of money – though in reality so many agencies charge much more than you do. Then, of course, I thought, "If she changes my way of life, this isn't expensive." ' She went on to describe how she had always wanted an outdoor life, and so for ten years she worked at a garden centre. When she was about twenty-four she got married, but it was a disaster because he was such a womaniser. By the time she was twenty-nine he had brought the marriage to an end through his constant affairs. In her earlier years with him they had tried to have a baby, but nothing happened. Eventually they got around to trying with IVF, as she was so desperate, but that didn't work either. A year or two went by after her separation and she felt very lonely. She would meet other men and think that maybe this was the one, only to be really disappointed when she got to know them better. Sometimes she'd think it wasn't worth meeting men because the constant disappointment made her feel even worse. She told me that when she got in touch with me she was very despondent. But then she added, 'You've got to keep going and trying. You've got to be optimistic. There must be someone out there for you.'

Jim said, 'In my mature years, now, I realise I wouldn't want to meet a woman who hadn't done something with her life. Pauline can certainly live independently from me – she doesn't want me for what she can get out of me, Sometimes I thought other women were trying that.'

The next time Jim went to Pauline's house he purposely sat in a single armchair to begin with – he didn't want her to think he was too forward. Then Pauline said, 'I thought he seemed a bit frosty, and I said to myself, "Well, he's got to shape himself up a bit because I can't be coping with a man who gives me no affection" – I'd had that for years previously.'

I remarked that I'd come across this attitude quite often. The men deliberately hold back in the amorous arena while the women say quietly to themselves, 'For God's sake come and get me.' Jim laughed and recalled how in his youth he had gone out with a girl for over a month before he even kissed her.

'I'd have ditched you,' said Pauline. We all laughed at this and said how much that showed that it always has to be the right person at the right time in anyone's life. Perhaps Pauline wouldn't have been right for Jim if he had met her twenty years previously.

That third time when Jim came over to her house Pauline asked, when it got late in the evening, if he wanted to stay over. His reply was, 'No, no, no, no – no.' Jim then asked a while after if the offer was still there, to which Pauline replied that he could have her bed and she would have the settee. James then said that he only really wanted her bed if she was in it too. With a twinkle and a giggle from both, the atmosphere was relieved by Pauline saying it was a deal. She continued, 'I've always felt that if your sex life is good together then so many things that could be difficult will be overcome much more easily. We found it so wonderful – for the first time we experienced the warmth and affection that we had both gone so long without. Something far more precious than sex developed between us that night – mutual bonding with great tenderness.'

I asked Jim about his farm, and he told me he had been born and brought up in the old farmhouse. His father was a farmer, and they ran a dairy herd until Jim damaged some cartilage in his knee and his doctor advised him to give up livestock. So they went arable. At that time they had just over 200 acres – tiny by today's standards. After his dad died in 1987 James decided to expand, and he now had 320 acres. He had had to pay £200,000 a short while back for his divorce settlement. 'I'm sure this affects a lot of farmers today. They are very wary of getting into a committed relationship, knowing that if they have to go through a divorce a lot of money has to be found, given the large assets that owning land brings.'

He went on to say that when his mum is no longer there (she lives in a house close by) he felt radical changes would take place. He used to live to farm – but not any more. 'I'll retire and enjoy far more golfing afternoons – live off my interest. I doubt I'll be farming after I'm fifty-five.'

In November they had started making plans for Pauline to come over to Jim's farm for Christmas. One night, out of the blue, he had said, 'I could definitely live with you, you know. What about living together?' There was a silence after they told me this. Then they went on to say that on the phone that week it was mutually agreed that Pauline would give up her job to come and live with Jim.

On reflection, they realised they had only met seven times before deciding on this course of action. The day after Pauline had left her job Jim came with a van to take her and all her stuff over to the farm. By the end of that day Pauline's old home was empty. 'If you don't do something you never get anywhere,' she said. 'I thought, "What have I got to lose?" A dear friend of mine had just died. I was devastated and thought, "Life doesn't go on for ever. Go for it."'

Then I asked them to tell me about their life together now.

'Well, Jim can be old-fashioned and a bit fussy, but I just let him get on with it. Sometimes I'll admit that I miss my home that I spent such a lot of money on, but then when Jim comes back into the house I realise with a jolt how wonderful it is to have his love and companionship. What is the point of a superbly designed home if you have no one to share it with?'

Pauline gets on very well with his mother, who doesn't actually approve of them living together but has come to accept it. They visit her every day and most days she cooks a meal for them. 'It keeps her occupied and gives her something to look forward to,' said Jim. 'Oh, she's lovely,' added Pauline.

The one painful, sad aspect of their life, just at the time when they are experiencing so much joy together, is that Jim has had to face the fact that he has recently become father to a child whose mother, it seems, used him to get pregnant, then promptly left him, and has now dropped the bombshell that he has a baby daughter to support. Pauline wants to understand what Jim is going through with this. Whatever he decides, she will go with. Jim has never had other children, so Pauline realises that if she can't give him any children it will be his only chance.

'It's so unfair,' said Pauline. 'I would love this baby to be ours, or even be a little part of our lives in the future.' But it seems this won't happen, as the mother is demanding that Jim supports the child but isn't prepared to let him see her or have her in his life. She added, 'I would love to look after the baby some days, but I know that will never take place.' She and Jim have to face reality in this respect. It doesn't look as if they will have children together, and they have to come to terms with this sad fact.

But they are very positive about their life together. 'We've found it so wonderful, really. For years we had a yearning for true love. We know now that we've found it.' Then Pauline added, 'I joke sometimes in bed and remind him most days what good value for money he was!'

9
Quaint Old English Customs

Most of the winter months in farming are dull, dismal and cold, especially on our upland livestock farm where the work is toughest in winter and it doesn't turn into spring until quite late into the year. The occasional crisp, sunny day can be quite beautiful, but you are constantly looking forward to those first few signs of spring – be it buds on the trees, early daffodils, anything really which heralds that spring is just around the corner and that the dark days will soon be over, the fog will relent and the sun will feel wonderful on your back as you go about your business.

On these dreary, hard days I always think my main job is to keep everywhere warm, with abundant clean dry clothing and lots of hot food available. What an old-fashioned attitude, you're possibly saying to yourself, but for a farm and a farmer to work well and as profitably as possible you have to have these very basic essentials in place.

On the other side of the farmyard, in the bureau office, I leave all this domesticity behind and run what I hope has always been an efficient, effective little business.

You would think that no one's thoughts would turn to

love and romance in these cold months, but the atmosphere in the office in February is one of enthusiasm and hope. Amazingly, it always seems one of the busiest times of the year. I put it down to Christmas, when many people find themselves alone and don't want to be, so they decide to make an earnest effort in the weeks ahead. Or perhaps over Christmas an established relationship didn't live up to expectations and has now been brought to a close, with the hope that they will find a new love in the New Year.

I have always got quite a lot of publicity, from newspapers, TV and radio, in that dull period between New Year and spring. Maybe it's because the media are trying to push the romance and love angle to their readers and listeners and viewers to alleviate the depression of those dark winter days. And the arrival of Valentine's Day in mid-February usually has them looking for something to do with love and relationships. An article headlined 'Cut Price Brides', published by the *Daily Express* in 1986, was perhaps the most sensational in its opening lines, in that it emphasised to lonely Falkland Islanders that I was charging a very low price and therefore a good bargain was to be had by joining the bureau. 'Introducing the Introducer' was the title of an article published by the *British Farmer* magazine. When I look at the photo of me that accompanied it in 1983 I looked like a teenager – in fact I do recall giving them a picture of a younger me, which I suppose was quite naughty.

The *Yorkshire Post* did two long articles quite close

together. In 'A Farmer's Wife with a Unique Occupation', published in 1986, they wrote, curiously, that I was 'only accessible by a rough track through windswept fields'. A follow-up in 1989 stated that 'wedding invitations flutter in like confetti' and 'kittens frisk beneath the table closely followed by sheepdog Bess' – did we have a sheepdog called Bess? We certainly didn't have kittens under the kitchen table, as I can't abide cats and have always put any kittens in the engine shed where it's warm.

Going into the 1990s, the *Mail on Sunday* did a four-page article titled 'The Farmer Wants a Wife' for their Valentine's Day issue. Here they called me a 'jolly, roly-poly woman', but made up for this by doing some really good in-depth interviews with two bureau members from the south and two from the north.

In 1992 the magazine *Country Living* gave us two full pages based on interviews they had done with bureau members, also calling their article 'The Farmer Wants a Wife'. They described in depth the story of my client Andrew from Somerset, who was desperately lonely. Working very long hours and despairing that he would ever find anyone, he poured his heart out to the journalist. But it was frustrating to me, and possibly all of those people who read his story, that it was never followed up, because just one week later Andrew met through the bureau a lady whom he called his 'soulmate' and he has been really happy ever since.

Of all the national newspapers, the *Daily Telegraph* seems to have produced the most thorough articles on the agency, first in 1989 with 'Rural Course of True Love Given a Helping Hand' and then, using the now well-worn title 'The Farmer Wants a Wife', in 2002. For the first article they sent a photographer, who was most insistent that I sat on a stone wall with the wind coming at me at practically force ten. I was appalled that the whole nation would see me in this dreadful gale, hair even more untidy than it normally is. The second article, which was very well researched with thorough interviews of myself and clients, was my favourite. It was illustrated with a fabulous cartoon by 'Joe', who had drawn the stereotypical country bloke with mucky wellies and a flat cap, and by his side a buxom, busty wench with an apron around her ample middle. Lamb under one arm, pig under another, chickens flying in all directions, these two were striding across the farmyard blowing kisses to each other. You couldn't help but laugh your socks off at the impression it gave.

Some of the best articles have been in regional papers. I've had good coverage in the *Western Mail* with 'Cupid's Bow Aims at Farm Lonely Hearts', and 'Exclusive Matchmaking for Country Folk' appeared in the *Scottish Farmer* in 1992. They described me as 'warm and motherly as if nothing would surprise or annoy her'. So, what with the 'roly-poly' description and suggestions of being like a placid mother hen, I never did get my image of a vivacious sex goddess over to the public!

One of the most enjoyable interviews I have done was for the programme *Home Truths*, presented by John Peel. They asked if they could do a piece about the bureau, and said an interviewer would be in touch. When she telephoned she introduced herself by saying, 'You'll probably know me better as Ruth from *The Archers* – the wife of David Archer, one of the main characters.' I was indeed surprised, for the Geordie accent of the character she plays had been replaced by a well-spoken southern voice, which she told me was her real one. I asked if they had specifically arranged for her to interview me due to the farming connection. Apparently not. Doing general interviews for *Home Truths* was her second job.

When 'Ruth' arrived, I suppose I hadn't expected her to be so attractive, petite and dainty. I dived straight in to talk about farming, expecting her to be amazingly knowledgeable on agricultural matters as she is in her role in *The Archers*. But I was wrong here too.

'No, no,' she said. 'That's just for the radio. In fact I'd be delighted to come and watch John milk – it would be one of the few times I've been really close to cows!' I could hardly believe it, as she always comes over as the complete opposite on the radio and you are always hearing her in the milking parlour. What a fabulous actress!

She spent the whole day interviewing me, speaking with John, walking around the farm and getting to know the cows a bit better. She recorded the gurgling sounds of the milking machines in the parlour and the crunch of us walking over the fields and the crowing of our roaming cockerel searching his territory for another female to sexually exploit. The programme sounded brilliant when it was broadcast but, having been a devoted fan of *The*

Archers for many decades, I still can't believe that Ruth is the same un-farmish woman who visited me that day.

I've given three interviews on *Woman's Hour* over the twenty-years life of the bureau and spoken on numerous local radio shows. The one radio programme I refused to go on was the one hosted by Robin Day at 1 p.m. on Radio 4 – I know my place, and reckoned I would never be able to hold my own with him.

American, Canadian and Japanese television companies have all spent the day with me filming the bureau at work. The American company wanted to see the lives of 'typical English farmers who are looking for love'. I could only get one male bureau member to agree to be interviewed by them and I wouldn't countenance a fictitious interview, but the producer also wanted to see other clients doing their 'everyday farm work' and here I felt we could stretch the point. So we set up Charlie and Richard to be typical English farmers, each seeking a wife. I suppose we needed our heads examining, but when you're desperate needs must. They filmed Charlie feeding the cows in one part of the farm, then they filmed a close-up of him taking out his baccy tin and doing a roll-up, and finally leaning on a hay fork.

When it came to Richard's turn, off the producer went to another part of the farm to make it look like a different place owned by another farmer. John and I watched from afar, then nearly died a thousand deaths when they asked Richard if he could show them any typical English customs and he proceeded do a rendition of a Morris dance! Holding a stem of ragwort in each hand instead of the customary white handkerchiefs (he'd probably never owned one, let alone two, white handkerchiefs), he started dancing up and down, swaying and jumping as he went. Large and ample Richard was having the time of his life, and the producer just loved this 'quaint old English custom'. The programme was eventually shown coast to coast, and so the whole American continent must now think that all English farmers act as loony as they come and are constantly dancing about their farms with plants in both hands. Richard, I know, had visions of a wealthy American heiress being so smitten with him and his dancing that she would mail order for him to fly over to her instantly.

By the time Charlie and Richard had also acted their way through the Canadian film company's visit they seemed old hands at it. They considered it no different from their daily mucking out routine when the makers of a Japanese news programme stayed on the farm and filmed them. I understand the regulars at Richard's local were filled with wonder when he walked in and casually announced, when ordering his beer, that he had been on Japanese television that day.

I've been asked several times to appear on *Kilroy* and various chat shows to discuss 'the loneliness of the countryside'. I suppose the most exciting interview was in 1990 when I was interviewed live on *Wogan*. I was approached several weeks beforehand and arrangements were made for me to travel down for the day, stay in a hotel and have a limousine take me from the hotel to the television studios.

The day before I went to London the BBC telephoned to tell me who I would be appearing with on the programme. They told me it would be Bob Geldof and a pop group. They mentioned the name of the pop group but I'd never heard of them before and I didn't really take it in. I walked over to the farmhouse from the office and said to John and the children, 'I now know who I'm appearing with tomorrow. It's Bob Geldof and a pop group – I think they were called Water, Water, Water.' Ben and Sarah looked at me in completely silence for a few moments and then yelled, 'Mum, it's not Water, Water, Water – it's Wet, Wet, Wet! Oh, you're so daft, Mum – fancy not knowing them! Can we come, please, please, please?'

As I got ready for the show at the hotel I had been booked into I started to get very nervous. Then I told myself that if I continued in this vein I would make a complete hash of it and not enjoy the interview at all, so I made myself calm down. In due course the limousine arrived and I was driven to the theatre where the pro-gramme is recorded, to be greeted at the stage door by a crowd of autograph hunters. They were desperately disappointed when it was only me who got out of the car, but, had they known, would probably have given anything to swap places with me – I met Wet, Wet, Wet quite intimately, as they had to let me into their dressing room for a short while for me to undress slightly so the microphone could be put under my clothes. They were lovely boys, so easy and ordinary and friendly.

When I came out of make-up, I have to admit I looked

incredibly glamorous in comparison to my normal appearance, with a wondrous hairstyle and fabulous
amounts of mascara. In the hospitality room my nerves
were intact until some bright spark from the production
team reminded me that there could be an audience of 20
million out there! Suddenly I visualised everyone I'd ever
known in my life watching me, especially people I'd been
to school with and all my old boyfriends – I imagined all
the remarks that a particular old boyfriend I'd parted
from in acrimonious circumstances well over twenty
years ago could make. Then I convinced myself I would
reply in absolute gibberish to Wogan's questions and
began to dread the idea of being scrutinised by half the
population of the country watching TV. Fortunately
common sense kicked in and I decided that I must stop
this, and that I must treat him as a friend sitting beside me
talking in a normal way. When my turn came to be
interviewed everything went well and I enjoyed each of
my fifteen minutes of fame.

But what seems to stick in most people's memories is
the fact that I undressed in Wet, Wet, Wet's dressing
room!

10
Hearts and Flowers and Sleepless Nights

The Valentine season certainly brings romance to the forefront, and almost as soon as Christmas is over the greetings card industry has reminded us that, like it or not, love is in the air. One February I had a huge and elaborate bouquet delivered to my door on Valentine's Day. With overwhelming optimism I persuaded myself that John was keeping to a New Year's resolution that he had not told me about and was turning romantic in his old age. I should have known that those sort of miracles don't happen. The flowers weren't from my husband, but from the devoted suitor of a lady in Devon whom I had introduced a few months before. The note said that when he came to send his true love flowers for Valentine's Day, he thought about who had brought them together and felt that I deserved some just as much. What a lovely thought! He will obviously make a charming and romantic husband.

The lovely events of February tend to be engagements and weddings on Valentine's Day. I would have thought that people would aim for the warmer months, but to some of them getting married on this special day seems so right. Nearly every year on 14 February I have an invitation from somewhere in the country to attend a wedding. If they are far away I don't accept, but within a reasonable distance I certainly do.

In 2000 the BBC asked if they could feature the bureau in a Valentine's Day programme. I told them I'd be delighted, but that they would have to do the interview beforehand as I was going to a wedding that day and wouldn't be in the office. I could hear the cogs turning in their minds, and after a pause the producer asked, 'Would there be any chance of us coming along with you to this wedding, so we could do it as a special feature?'

'Oh! No, no, no – no, no,' I quickly said. 'They're a very shy couple who have led quiet lives. They'd never contemplate having their wedding televised.'

But the producer wouldn't take no for an answer, and asked me to put the idea to them and see what their reaction was.

Never in a million years would this particular couple want to have anything to do with television on such a day, I thought to myself. Reluctantly I picked up the phone, and when Howard answered it I very tentatively put the suggestion forward. He didn't know what to say at first – who would? Then he replied that he wasn't sure, it was a bit of a surprise, but if I hung on he'd ask Marie, his fiancée, who was standing right next to him. There was a lot of muttering in the background and I prepared myself for the expected polite apology. To my utter astonishment, however, when Howard came back on the line he said, 'We've decided we'll do it, Pat – just for you, especially if it would help other people like us get together.'

A little while later I discovered that representatives of three local newspapers were also going to be present because it was a Valentine's Day wedding. It still amazed me that this quiet, discreet couple had taken such a major step and said yes to all this publicity. 'What's the harm?' they both said. 'We're so proud to be marrying each other that we want the world to know.' They had already had a little experience of the media because in the autumn they had sent a letter to their local newspaper, the *Sentinel*, encouraging anyone who would be alone at Christmas to try to meet someone special through an introduction agency, and the paper printed the letter. The paper then got back in touch with them and said it would be pleased to feature them in the future and support the couple's wish to help or encourage other lonely, quiet people to join an agency and meet someone.

It was all set up for the presenter to arrive very early at the farm on Valentine's Day to interview me, after which they wanted to film me getting ready for the wedding and setting off. Somehow the local TV news programme, Central News, got wind of this as well and telephoned to ask if they could film the day's proceedings. 'In for penny, in for a pound,' I thought, and spoke again to Howard and Marie.

'Oh well, why not?' they said. 'We've led such a quiet and sheltered life, both of us – let's do it with a bang!'

The local hat shop in Bakewell, Lady Fair, are very

good. As I purchase so many wedding hats from them I always get a little discount and a good selection. On this occasion I bought a really special one to go with a new outfit as I thought I'd better look spruced up if we were all going to be on television. I had arranged for someone to come into the farmhouse the morning of the wedding to look after the film crew and interviewer and give them breakfast and coffee while I went and changed for the wedding. Everything had been organised to the last detail and I was all ready to go to bed early.

However, as John returned from his final check of his stock he announced that things didn't look too good for a peaceful night. It seemed we had two cows that might calve in the night. I couldn't believe this, as I couldn't remember a time ever when we had had two cows calving together in the night. So I put my head on my pillow muttering that I needed a good night's sleep and don't those cows understand. 'All may go well,' John replied. 'But I've got to go back out in an hour.'

Just as I was slumbering nicely John came upstairs and announced he needed my help. It wasn't the calving cows that were in trouble, but one that had already calved. She unexpectedly needed to be transferred to another shed and he couldn't do it alone. I got up and dressed and trundled behind John in my old warm coat that had done such good service on so many other similar cold dark nights – the same one, indeed, that I had worn when avoiding my best-dressed customer with the pram: the bag lady style, with the baler twine trim. Unknown to me it had started to snow, so the difference at half past midnight between my warm cosy bed and this trip to the cowshed was beyond belief.

We transferred the cow quite well, considering she had to do what cows hate – walk outside in a snowstorm. But immediately she arrived in her new quarters she collapsed with milk fever, which can often happen when a cow is giving lots of milk, usually just after calving. It is caused by a drastic drop of body calcium, which can very quickly become fatal if you don't give them an intravenous transfusion of calcium solution. It was time to act fast, but as John was administering the medication the cow lashed out and kicked me, flinging me several feet away and knocking me unconscious!

'Come on, Pat,' I heard as I came round. 'No time to be lying down on the job – we've got problems with those calvers now.' I know I saw stars that night – and they weren't only in the sky! Still, I managed to recover and went off to look at the calving cows. Sure enough, one needed our help. I don't have tremendous skills where calving is concerned, so I get relegated to the navvy status of fetcher, carrier and, in years gone by before we had mechanical help to aid calving, puller. (That meant pulling on two ropes which had been tied around the calf's ankles as they just poked out of the mother. You pulled like hell – you forgot your bad back, or that you might have the flu, or that your arms felt as if they would tear apart, and just kept pulling with all your might.) I went and fetched the calving aid that had replaced the heaving method and we began the task that we had done together for many years, John and I, in the middle of the night –

bringing life to a new little creature. Thankfully all went well, although it seemed to be a long job and by now it was about 2 a.m.

On our way back to the house we went to look at the second calving cow and could't believe it – she was in difficulties as well. So back I went to fetch the calving aid and start all over again. This time things proved very difficult. 'It's no good, we'll have to get the vet,' said John. Once again I thought how I needed my sleep in order to appear on telly later that day! But no matter how much you protest to yourself or to the Almighty it has no effect, so I went into the house to phone the vet.

Chris came out from Youlgrave, our local village, at about 3 a.m. I waited at the yard entrance to wave him in and direct him to the appropriate shed, having fetched hot water and clean towels (yes, you really do need the proverbial hot water when birthing difficult calves). An examination revealed that a caesarean was the only option. I went straight into my routine mode of fetching – a halter for the cow, more bales of straw to turn the surrounding area into a more hygienic working environment and a clean surface for the vet to put his implements on and more hot water. In the days of Chris's predecessor a bottle of whisky would have been requested as well. From long experience we all knew where to stand, and how to assist in the sterilisation of the wound area and other parts of the surgical procedure. A good healthy live heifer calf was born that night, but by the time everything was cleared away it was 4 a.m.

You always feel you have to invite the vet into the

house to clean himself up and once there you have to ask him if he'd like some coffee, no matter how tired you are. Of course if he's worked really hard you feel duty bound to offer something to eat as well. But for once, just once, I thought maybe we wouldn't – not that morning, because at least then I could have about an hour's sleep. Lo and behold, however, my dear benevolent husband asked, 'Are you going to have some breakfast with us before you go, Chris?' This was the one time that I crossed my fingers and hoped hard that our lovely vet would say no. Sod's law decreed that he said, 'Eh, that'd be grand.'

John smiled at me as if I'd been blessed to have this task allocated to me. Of course, had we not had company I would have delighted in telling him what a burk he was to suggest I should reach for the frying pan, on this of all days – didn't he know I needed some sleep? It was no good, however. I realised that, and so with a smile on my face I started getting a full English breakfast for the household. John always gets up to start milking at 5 a.m. When that time came the two men walked out, John to the cowshed, Chris to go home, while I was left to ponder on the fact that the TV cameras would be descending on me at 7 a.m. and I had had no sleep at all!

I decided not to think about this, but to look forward to the day. I felt the kitchen could be cleared and tidied by the lady who was coming in to attend to the film crew. Maybe I could close my eyes and doze for a while in the chair. But you know what it's like when you're over-tired and you know you can only shut your eyes for a short period – everything just keeps going over and over in your mind. I started thinking about Howard and Marie who were to be married that day, and hoping they had had their beauty sleep, because this was going to be the biggest event in their lives. As I rested I recalled the details of how they got together, and their whole story came into my mind all over again.

II

The Lonely Furrow

When Marie joined the bureau, her photograph showed her as a slim lady in her early fifties with twinkling eyes accompanying a lovely warm smile. She was short in stature, really no more than five feet, with grey hair that was nicely styled. Her nursing career had spanned thirty years, and she had been through a number of positions from practising midwife to ward sister before taking early retirement.

She lived in Nottinghamshire and, although her parents weren't farmers, many of her family were. Most of all she loved living in the countryside, hated towns and cities and seemed to have a very adaptable nature. She was obviously a caring person, but I couldn't get over the fact that she hadn't had a boyfriend for thirty years and even then she had only gone out with someone for a few months and it had not developed into a serious relationship. 'How could someone so lovely have slipped through the net?' I thought – and after all these years of being unattached, would she ever be able to develop a loving partnership with someone? Many people who have remained single into their forties and certainly fifties think they want that committed permanent relationship, but when it comes down to it, when they really have to face the fact of having someone else constantly in their life, a long-standing single person cannot always accept this change. But you don't know until you try, so of course I set to work with Marie and decided to do my best.

When Howard joined, which was about two months after Marie, I didn't rush to 'match' him up instantly as I was going on holiday. On the beach one day, in a relaxed moment of letting any sort of thought drift into my mind, as one does, I started to think about Howard and who I could introduce to him. While looking out to sea I thought of Marie, and kept her image firmly in my mind for when I returned home to my office.

So, on starting work again after the break, the first introduction I considered was Marie and Howard. I had spoken at length to both, but not met either of them at that stage. I deliberated in my office, with Howard's form in one hand and Marie's in the other. Marie was only two months older than Howard, so the age seemed fine, but he was considerably taller – about 14 inches taller actually, which most people feel is too much of a difference. Tall men – those over six feet – usually prefer taller women, and I like to keep men of this height for ladies of five feet ten and over.

Howard was a well-built man with glasses, hair a bit receding – not too distinguished, you might say; but he had a lovely, friendly, smiley face and looked a very sincere man. They were not a great distance from each other, Howard in Staffordshire and Marie in

Nottinghamshire. The most amazing aspect of their potential match was that Howard had written down that he had never had a girlfriend, just as Marie had revealed to me that she had also never had a serious boyfriend.

Well, maybe they could learn together: I sent the introductions out. For several months, all went quiet. If I don't hear anything at the beginning of an introduction I leave well alone, which is what I did here. My clients know I'm always there to help or advise, but I never interfere unless asked. Then out of the blue Howard telephoned one day and said that he and Marie would very much like me to visit them both, preferably at his place. It was February 1999 and he said they really would like me to come on Valentine's Day, if possible. I thought they must have something going to ask me to meet them together, but obviously had no idea of the extent of the relationship.

I arrived at Howard's home in the early afternoon to be greeted at the farm gate by two small, furry dogs, who were quite yappy but seemed friendly enough. I left the car on the drive and walked up to the bungalow, a small, neat place with a few farm buildings around it. The door opened as I put up my hand to knock, revealing two of the friendliest-looking people I'd ever encountered. The smiles from both were as wide and happy as you could get, and both exuded a warmth that enveloped me instantly.

I was ushered into their cosy living room and settled into a comfy armchair. The signs looked good, and I thought maybe I'd cracked it again here. After they had both sat down on the settee opposite we started to chat about this and that. Eventually I asked them to tell me how they felt about my bureau and matchmaking, and whether it had worked for them. It was obviously going to take a while for them to come to the point of why they had asked me to visit.

Howard then proceeded to tell me that he had actually written off for my brochure about seventeen years previously, but never in all that time had he plucked up the courage to go through with joining. This staggered me. I asked him what had finally pushed him to get in touch with me.

The last straw, apparently, was that he had answered yet another personal ad in the local paper and been let down yet again. He had met this lady once, when she was on her way home, in a car park. They had arranged to meet again at a theatre, but she didn't turn up and then he couldn't get her on the telephone. Her daughter used to answer the phone, saying to Howard, 'Me mam isn't in.' This went on for about six weeks. He continued, with a marked sadness in his tone, 'Anyway, I felt so let down that I decided that I wasn't going to do anything other than through a third party in future. I was so hurt and disappointed.' The rejection came through in his voice. 'How little we all realise,' I thought, 'how massive the hurt can be to someone when we dismiss them so easily.'

He continued, 'I was off work for a while after that with bad back pain' – he worked part-time as a driver for a local company. 'With being off work I'd go for days upon days without actually seeing anybody. I used to go up to town, and the girls at the checkout in the super-market wouldn't speak. You just get your food, pay your money and come back out again, and you can actually return home without having had a conversation with anyone. The only person who would speak to me was the one at the chip shop. I wasn't supposed to have fish and chips really, but I was getting to the stage where, if I wanted to talk to somebody for a few minutes, I'd go and buy a packet of chips and throw them away when I got home. I just wanted so much to speak to someone. That was about the only hope I had of having anyone to talk to.'

The total despondency of that time showed so obviously in his face that I wanted to get up and comfort him. 'Christmas came,' he went on, 'and for three days I never saw a soul, let alone spoke to anyone. When I was doing my driving job I never came across female company much at all – it's such male-orientated work. Usually I was taking cement on to building sites, where there are only men.'

There must be women out there looking for companionship be reckoned, but where to make contact with them. 'I knew the lady I was looking for was sitting at home somewhere by herself like me. I knew I wouldn't find her in a pub or anything like that. I did used to go to the theatre occasionally, but it was always on my own, and you could go there and back again without speaking to anybody. People would be in groups or couples, and I would never want to push my company on anyone who didn't want it. Even if you see a woman in a group with other lady friends, you don't know if they've got a partner or not. I found it an impossible situation.'

Marie broke in: 'People who aren't in a situation like Howard don't realise, do they, this state of absolute loneliness? And of course Howard wasn't the only one. I was doing similar things over in the next county, because I was so lonely. One thing we both found out was that for years we have both kept the radio on throughout the night. You can't stand the continual silence, so with a radio on at least you feel you have someone with you in the night.'

Howard continued, 'I'd seen your adverts in the papers – I think it used to be in the *British Farmer*, or other farming papers. But then I'd think to myself no one would ever want to be with me, so I never dared approach you. I suppose I've got a terrible inferiority complex. I thought over the years that I wasn't worth anything to anybody. I felt I'd never had anything but rejection all my life, even as a child. I've been approaching ladies for a date since before I was twenty, but I went for ten or thirteen years without even asking anybody out because I couldn't stand being constantly rejected. Anyway, I was so disappointed that I could hardly ever get a date from the newspaper adverts that I decided I wouldn't bother with them again, but I'd go to Mrs Warren's bureau – a third party, so as to know where I stood.'

His decision was reinforced by a relative, he told me. 'You know you fixed up my cousin Diane's daughter to a man called Malcolm, an agricultural engineer? I used to ring Diane and she said to me one night, "Howard, why don't you join Mrs Warren's bureau?" It stuck in my mind, and I couldn't think of a reason why not.

'In my dreams, I'd always wanted to meet a nurse. Maybe it's because they're caring people and a nurse wouldn't mock you or reject you casually, because she'd understand the hurt. When the paperwork came on Marie and I saw she was a nurse I was overwhelmed, and I have to admit I cried.' As he finished his story his face revealed the utter disbelief that she had come into his life.

I turned to Marie to enquire how she had come to join the bureau, and she told me it was through her local veterinary practice. 'They insisted – the vets and all the nurses – that I got in touch with you, because they thought my life was being wasted. They got all the papers for me and filled everything out and just said, "Sign here." It's taken me a lifetime to feel I can trust anyone – I lost all my confidence for years and years after a very short relationship ended, when my boyfriend told me he was gay. I couldn't regain my self-esteem and I just threw myself into my career, and then my mother became ill and after that my father and I had to look after them. I loved them so much – I just wish they could have met Howard. I know my dad would have got on with him. Afterwards, when I was completely alone, I just got more and more depressed. Finally my dog died, and I really went into a decline then. So I decided to finish work as a midwifery sister.'

Howard picked up the thread: 'You know, the similarities in our lives before we met are immense. Although they were different situations, the same emotions were involved with both of us, so we do understand what each other has gone through.' Marie put her arm through Howard's as they sat on the sofa together and declared, 'My confidence has only been restored by this wonderful man.'

I asked Howard to tell me a little about his earlier life. He told me that he'd bought a piece of land off his dad before he sold the main farm so that at last he'd got something of his own, independent from the family, and built this small bungalow. He described how he had always reared livestock, but started to go lorry driving as well to bring in a regular income. As I looked around I took in the glorious views from the bungalow, with one side leading down to a lake and the undulating country-side of north Staffordshire on the other. His acreage was small, but Howard was never going to be into big-time farming and he said he was happy that way. Through the large picture window I could see about twenty good, strong-looking bullocks.

I asked them both to tell me their first impressions when they started speaking to each other on the phone. Marie told me that she thought what a lovely, sincere, trusting voice Howard had. They didn't meet straight-away, but had a number of phone calls over several weeks.

For their first meeting Howard suggested Carsington Reservoir, a lake and leisure complex halfway between them, as they both knew where that was. Then they started giggling, and Howard said, 'But we were in a mess really, because there's about a thousand car park spaces there, you see, and I got the last one. It was Easter weekend, so a million other people were there that afternoon.'

With great hilarity, mocking themselves for choosing such a silly day when half the population of the Midlands was there as well, Marie explained how she had had to keep driving around all the car parks and had already walked around all the cars but couldn't see his registration number – and in any case apparently he'd got that wrong! They both laughed at the ridiculous situation that they had got into, and we agreed it was a miracle they ever even met.

Howard thought the only thing he could do was sit in his car and wait, and Marie said she just kept driving round until eventually she saw a red Volvo such as he'd described. A man got out, but she couldn't really look at him as she still hadn't found anywhere to park. Eventually they both managed to be stationary at the same time, so Howard walked over and suggested she should follow him to the nearby village of Tissington. Apparently he hadn't even asked her if she was Marie! But the problem now was that they were holding all the traffic up. They both laughed uproariously again at the memory, and Marie admitted that she hadn't got a clue where she was driving when she started to follow Howard that afternoon.

Howard recalled, 'The first thing she said to me when we eventually parked up was that I was handsome – can you believe that? Me handsome? No one had ever in the whole of my life told me that before. And we were holding hands within two minutes – it was lovely. Then we found a tearoom and I think I fell in love with her while we were having a cup of tea and I thought to myself, "I'm not going to let this one slip through the net."' As they snuggled up to each other and gazed into each other's eyes you could tell that they were truly and deeply in love, just like a couple of teenagers.

Marie then told me she had cried all the way home because she thought Howard wouldn't want to see her again. She described how much she had liked him, and she knew she could love him because he was sincere and just the type of person that she wanted to love. The atmosphere was full of emotion at this point, particularly from Marie. Her arm went through his and she touched him gently on the cheek, perhaps to reassure herself that all this was truly taking place and that he was real flesh and blood.

Howard took up the tale: 'We spoke on the phone again and arranged to meet up next in the centre of Ashbourne. Marie had suggested we meet in the car park in the centre of town. Well, I waited for three hours against that stone statue in the middle of Ashbourne. I kept buying car parking tickets, but then I decided this was no good and I drove over to where she lived in Nottinghamshire. It was a bit of a struggle because I didn't know the way. Anyway, I did manage to get there eventually.'

Marie said, 'When he arrived I was in tears because I'd

just got back from driving all around Ashbourne and I hadn't seen Howard at all and thought he just hadn't bothered to turn up. I couldn't believe that he'd put himself out enough to drive all that way to come to see me! I was overwhelmed. Of course, that was the first time we'd been able to relax and really get to know each other. It was wonderful. The first time in my life that someone wanted me – wanted me for me, and not for what I could do for them.'

Howard wanted Marie to spend a weekend with him, but she couldn't as she had no one to look after her dogs – she couldn't really leave her home for more than a couple of hours. 'I'd got eight dogs at the time. I'd taken in strays to compensate for my loneliness, you see. I finished up, I suppose, being a prisoner in my home, and I didn't realise that until Howard told me. One dog was paranoid about Howard when he came. He wouldn't leave him, constantly jumping up at him and barking, and some of them were very jealous of him coming on to the scene. Howard told me that I'd been so good to them, that I'd reared them and saved them from the needle, but that they'd grown up and needed homes of their own now. I listened to every word he said, right from then, because I know when somebody's talking common sense and I knew he was telling me the truth. But I never intended keeping all the dogs anyway, so I managed to find homes for all of them except the two here today.' They both laughed at their recollection of this predicament. Shortly afterwards Marie visited Howard's farm, where she not only fell in love with its owner but was immediately smitten with the little house and the surrounding countryside.

When Howard went to stay for his first weekend at Marie's, it was the first time he'd stayed away from his home since he was about fifteen or sixteen. 'I had the biggest job to persuade myself to get in the car and come away from here. It took an hour or two. I'd got my bags packed, but I just couldn't get used to not being here. I'd checked all the doors and windows and plugs two or three times and made sure I'd locked up and I'd got everything, but even then I found it very difficult – it was only sheer determination to achieve what I wanted, to love Marie and make a life with her and get rid of the sheer loneliness and despair for ever, that got me away from here.

'I wanted to keep the love I had for Marie to myself for a while – I suppose I was worried it would all fall through – but she wanted me to ring my mother up. I said, "I've got a new friend," and she replied, "What's his name?" I don't know whether they were thinking I'd got a boy-friend or what. That's the danger when you're single at our age – everybody thinks you're gay. Of course, I put her right straightaway and described Marie to her. She seemed thrilled – in fact it's a long time since I've know my mother get so excited. I only told one person after that and that was Edgar, and it was a complete surprise to him. He used to work for my dad before I was born. I knew I didn't have to tell anybody else. I just said to him, "Don't tell anybody", and I knew that would seal it. Edgar would tell everybody.'

Both then explained that Marie used to come and stay for weekends once she had found good homes for the dogs. She would spend a few days with Howard, then go home and be totally miserable, while Howard for his part would be miserable without her. Then one day Howard put his foot down and said he didn't want her to be living by herself any more – so she moved in.

'The biggest excitement the neighbours had was the day a new double bed arrived at my front door. They all got to know about it, as the furniture men couldn't find the place and asked at one or two other farms down the road for directions. So the arrival of the double bed spread like wildfire around the locality within a few hours,' Howard proudly exclaimed.

He then said, 'Sometimes when I'm outside, and I look back at this bungalow, I can't believe the gem I've got inside now. I used to be up the fields, before I met Marie, and I'd walk back down to the bungalow and perhaps it'd be dark and there'd be no light on, or the curtains would be open and there'd be no one moving about, and it looked empty and dead. I used to despair with the loneliness and weariness. It was terrible. I would look through my photograph album virtually every day for companionship.'

But now life has changed so much, and they have found perfect contentment in each other. 'It's so beautiful here,' Marie said. 'The countryside, even to see a mouse running around, or the hares in the field, the change of the seasons. You know, we're both crazy about the English countryside. We don't need foreign holidays at all because we don't need to escape, especially now we've got each other. Everything we need is here.'

Marie revealed that hiding under that quiet exterior was the kindest, loveliest man you could ever wish to meet, and added that no one knew in all those years that he wrote poetry and has the most wicked sense of humour. She explained she sometimes has to beg him to stop telling jokes and imitating people, as 'I just can't stop laughing.'

Howard told me more about the degree to which his life had changed. 'One day we went with some friends of Marie's to a farm where a Lancaster bomber was being rebuilt, and all the engines were running and we had a ride on it. The same friends took us to the coast that day. I realised that it was the first time I'd been to the coast for about thirty-five years. The last time I remember seeing the sea was on a day trip to Blackpool when I was about twenty-one.'

Marie said, 'The greatest sadness I have is that we didn't both come to you when we were much younger, because I would so much like to have had Howard's children, and now it's too late. I sometimes try to imagine what they'd have been like, but if we could encourage other single people to do the same as we've done that would be so good. Because loneliness is by far the most terrible thing that ever happens to anyone.'

I said to both, 'It strikes me, sitting here and listening to you, what a sensible, down-to-earth couple you are, because out of the blue, without ever having had to handle the emotional aspects of a relationship, there you are at the helm of this ship, steering things so well.'

Howard went quite serious and said, 'We want you to be the first to know, Pat, as it's all come about through you, that today, with you by our side, we would like to get engaged.'

'Wow!' I thought. 'This is quite something – this is the stuff that fairy tales are made of.' Before I could continue with my thoughts Howard had got a little box out of his pocket. He opened it, took out a pretty diamond ring, turned to Marie and, holding her hand, said to her, 'You are everything in the world to me. I cannot imagine my life without you now or ever.' With that he slipped the ring on to her left hand and said, 'You were worth waiting thirty years for.' The kiss that followed was filled with such love and devotion that my heart nearly burst with joy at witnessing this magical scene on Valentine's Day 1999.

One year on, as I dozed in my chair on Valentine's morning 2000, this lovely couple's wedding day, I realised I could not slumber any more and would have to get a move on. I showered and changed from my smelly farm clothes into a sober suit suitable for an interview by the BBC. In due course the interviewer asked me about my work and then, while the film crew had some breakfast, I changed into my wedding outfit and the TV crew filmed me as I was doing my hair and putting on my wedding hat. Then it was a dash to the wedding venue to set up their cameras.

I was scheduled to arrive at Howard's farm a short

while before Marie was due to set off. It was a good job I had to drive through the fresh air of the Staffordshire moorlands, for after my night assisting cows in labour I certainly needed something to liven me up. Marie, very excited, had just finished getting ready. She was full of laughter as she always is, but like all brides quite awe-struck at what she was about to do. She wore a lovely misty pastel green and cream dress with a cream coat, topped with a big picture hat in the beautiful colours of her dress, and carried an exquisite bouquet of flowers in pastel mint, lemon and cream. She looked radiant, and I certainly told her so. All the time she was getting ready she had had a TV news crew filming the beginning of her special day.

Howard seemed to be nowhere around, but I believe he was at the next farmhouse to the west. The farmer to the east arrived in his splendidly ribbon-bedecked car to take Marie to the wedding service. It was to be a real little country wedding and we all set off for the ceremony in the wake of the film crew. Excitement mounted when we reached our destination because the police had closed the road as there were so many reporters and TV crews around.

The music 'The Power of Love' was played at the beginning of the ceremony, and by the end there wasn't a dry eye in the house. Even the hardened TV and news-paper reporters were emotional as they filmed them coming out as man and wife. A man came up to me on the pavement and said, 'Is it really true that Howard's getting married here today? Well, I never! I was told in town this morning that this was happening, but I couldn't believe it, so I had to come and see for myself.' At that point Marie and Howard appeared being showered with confetti, looking radiantly happy.

The TV news crew then rushed away as they wanted to show the wedding film on the lunchtime Valentine news programmes. The rest of us drove to the reception several miles away in the countryside. It's always the same when I attend wedding receptions – I get the feeling they really don't know where to put me. Which side, bride or bridegroom, do I sit? Who do I sit by? I know when couples invite me they tend to feel I should have quite a high-priority seat, but as to how or where the etiquette books don't yet cater for someone like me. Once, at a wedding in East Anglia, I was placed next to a bishop – that, I suppose, was quite prestigious. Mostly I seem to be seated next to a special aunt, but this time I was placed next to Howard's eldest brother, Edward and sister-in-law.

He said to me, 'It's quite incredible – I still can't believe that it's our Howard here today with all these TV film crews and newspapers. He's been so very quiet all his life. We knew nothing at all about this romance, you know, until just over a month before they got engaged. Then one Saturday night I was having a bath and my wife appeared with a newspaper.' She took over the tale: 'I always read the *Sentinel* of a Saturday night, and as I was glancing through I started to read a letter a couple had sent in. I read who it was from, and thought, "I'm misreading this – I'll have to go and get my glasses."

When I put my glasses on, it read the same. It was from Howard, telling of his love for this lady. I was speechless. I had to go straight up to Edward to show him, and we just couldn't take it in.' I smiled to myself as I heard all this, and thought how wonderful that life can still be full of surprises.

The reception went beautifully, with great goodwill and laughter. Everyone had a good time, and Marie and Howard left with everyone's warmest wishes for their future. They didn't have a honeymoon. They said they just wanted to be in their home together and look after the twin goats that had been born that morning on the farm.

12
A Tall Order

I can think of nothing more annoying when you join an introduction agency than having someone constantly bombarding you with advice and pushing their own feelings and approach to life on to you when you don't need it and certainly don't want it. My aim has been never to give advice until it is asked for, and I always work to that principle. However, many people are very apprehensive and may be a little confused about how to go about meeting someone through an agency; this applies particularly to shy, retiring people who lead rural lives. Most city dwellers are used to communicating on many levels, but for that quiet country person who doesn't mix with many people and possibly doesn't have a lot of friends around their own age it can seem a daunting prospect. The middle pages of the bureau brochure contain advice which a member can digest and take on board if they want to.

In it I outline methods of getting to know each other, I warn against trying to rush into a relationship, and I encourage my clients to have a positive outlook towards their eventual success. Romance will come along when you least expect it. That really is a saying I definitely believe in, and there is a very curious but quite common phenomenon that bears out my belief. A bureau member will come for an interview. They will tell me how they've been trying to meet someone special for years and years. They then say, 'Now I've joined you, everything will be all right. I'm sure you'll find me someone.' This is very unnerving, because although it's good that they have faith in the bureau I worry that they feel all their woes in life will now be solved. However, what has happened so many times is that only a few weeks after that person has gone home I get a call from them, and in embarrassed tones they inform me that since joining the bureau they have, amazingly, met someone without my help and a simple friendship seems to be leading into a special relationship. They can't believe it, and certainly can't understand how they can go for years without developing a relationship but, as soon as they put themselves into my hands, do so.

I think that's the essence of it all. Once they've done something positive such as joining a bureau, in their minds they say, 'Right, that's fixed, that's done, there's no need for me to try any more. The bureau is going to do everything for me in the romantic department' – and they relax. Once they are relaxed and stop giving off an aura of desperately seeking a mate, casual meetings with other people become considerably more stress-free. They don't try because there's no need to try – the bureau is going to do it all for them. And with this softer attitude, romance seems to come through the door when they least expect it.

One of the great things about dealing with different sorts and conditions of people in the office is that you can have the most intriguing conversation when you least expect it. Something that I least expect, but are increasing in number, are calls from gay men and women who want to know if I can help them. I'd like to able to say I can help anyone at all who lives in the countryside, no matter what their orientation, but at the moment I just cannot help this minority group simply because that's exactly what it is. There are so few people who approach me with this issue that, even if I did form a sub-section of my main register for them, their choice with me would be too small, and a gay person needs to have as much choice in an introduction as a heterosexual person. I do advise them, though, to join an agency called Significant Others, which has a good reputation in the introduction industry.

How life changes. Twenty years ago I would never have had calls from gay people, but of course it's good that they can now be so much more open. As we all know, life has changed in terms of women's expect-ations. So often I'm asked by a man to find 'someone just like my mother'. To which my reply is that there will never be anyone the same as your mother and nowadays many women want a completely different lifestyle any-way – independence, an ability to make decisions rather than have their husbands do all that for them, and the wish to make a financial contribution to the family usually by going off the farm to work. So the stereo-typical farmer's wife who stays at home all day, baking bread and making jam, with masses of children running at her feet and chickens scratting around just outside the farmhouse door, is rapidly becoming less of a reality. I'm all in favour of women having greater choices in life, but I do sometimes wonder whether some women don't lose out on quality of life when they are juggling their lives as wives, mothers and income providers, trying to keep everything up in the air but not knowing when one element or another will fall and perhaps never be happily recaptured.

When discussing the changing make-up of human society I'm at times asked to comment on my feelings about actual marriage in the future. Who can say? Maybe things will reverse and marriage will become more popular again, but possibly not. I do think that more and more people will be reluctant to enter into the implications of marriage without living together first, and it's the old-fashioned pattern of engagement, marriage and then living together which will be unusual.

One thing I've found with some modern women is that they don't try to be feminine at all. They think it's quite wrong to bow to a man's wish to be with a girly, feminine lady. Little do they realise that one of the main criteria for most men who ask me about a woman is if she is feminine. A female client will ask me, 'What do you think I should wear on my first date?' I'll reply, 'Maybe a skirt would be good', and they will come back with, 'Never. I always wear trousers.' But sometimes introductions like that go wonderfully well, and I will certainly be put in my place for being so sceptical.

I've been proved wrong about many things, of course.

There can be no hard and fast rules, because as soon as you try to set some down human nature comes along and throws them aside. Sometimes I'm reluctant to accept a particular person on to the register. I would never feel this lack of enthusiasm because someone was physically unattractive, but I can recall instances when I've thought a person was too miserable or had what I thought was the wrong attitude. Sometimes life has given me a bit of a jolt in these circumstances, and I recall two clients who I thought would not easily form attachments but whose first introductions proved absolutely successful.

One lady I interviewed had no smile or humour, no warmth in her at all. Yet within weeks of giving her the first introduction the man let me know he was deliriously in love with her and was going to ask her to marry him. She didn't bother to phone me, but he has always kept in touch and I believe they are still happily married. Isn't it amazing?

The second instance was a very masculine woman who came for an interview. In fact, when she walked in, had I not previously received her registration form I would not have guessed her gender. She was incredibly well educated and I thought this would daunt most of the men on my register. Nevertheless the first introduction proved blissfully successful, instantly. Although they aren't yet married I have had letters from both declaring their devotion and love for each other. When this happens I concede that I don't know everything – both these unexpected relationships certainly put me in my place and taught me a thing or two. Once again I bow down and pay homage to the incredible power of human nature.

The power of the human spirit was certainly put to test in the agricultural world in the early spring of 2001, when foot and mouth disease was diagnosed in some parts of the country. Some bureau members who were in the middle of the whole awful business went silent for weeks. They couldn't venture off their farms and their stock had been killed, and afterwards some of them told me they were in such shock that they couldn't raise their bodies or even their heads to look forward to another day. Some literally went to bed for days. They couldn't take in that all their livestock had been culled, especially if the animals didn't have the disease but were just contacts. Of course, the men on my register were usually living by themselves with no wife or girlfriend for support. To some I did become that much-needed crutch, and occasionally grown men would weep uncontrollably down the phone. I would just listen and then try very hard to get them to look to the idea of a future. I felt at least I had done my little bit to help in this whole dreadful episode.

Gradually, as the year progressed from those dreadful days of February and March, we went into spring, life started to get back to normal a little, and life had to go on. Foot and mouth carried on all summer, but we all tried to develop an optimistic outlook on life.

Springtime, for me, always brings hope for the year ahead and I'm sure this sentiment is true for most people. I get up with greater enthusiasm than on the dreary, dark winter mornings and I have a definite 'spring' in my step, delighted to be up and doing in the early morning sunshine (though please don't visualise me doing a May Day dance naked in the early morning dew. It wouldn't be a pretty sight!) It was on one of these early spring days that I met up again with a couple who had joined the bureau in the previous year.

Sarah was such a sincere person, full of passion for what she believed in, but she expressed that enthusiasm within a calm and mellow nature. Before she came for an interview at the office she had obviously thought about the ramifications of joining the bureau very seriously and wrote me a letter saying:

I'm not a complicated person. From my early years I just wanted to continue farming into my adult life. I am a farmer's daughter, so I know what the life is like. I am quite strong and dependable workwise, and able to work through problems and be strong throughout difficult days. I would just like to get on with jobs that need doing and build something good with a special person. I realised two or three years ago that I was never going to settle in a non-farming world.

Other people have told me that this is a naïve and romantic idea and have said to me – one day you will grow up. If my dreams were to come true the falling-in-love bit would be to a kind and warm-hearted man, a bit boyish and tall, easy-going, who would see fun in so many things. He would not be over-ambitious. A man with an easy nature, who smiled often, with kind eyes.

He would respect people and all their differences. I would like to be able to laugh with him easily at things that happen in day-to-day life. He would be very practical and not too serious. He would possibly have a small farm, which he loved, and this would be his world and he would be content with it and with the local area. He would work hard and he would be a person who could see the greater picture of life and humanity in this world. He would be open-minded and he would not be driven to wanting a high material lifestyle or wanting to travel all over the place. I imagine a basic farmhouse that is very practical – not showy, but cosy. Knowing me, I would possibly be trying to get a small farm venture off the ground. It would be something like chickens and eggs, it would not be big business. I would just basically love this life.

When she appeared at the bureau office I noticed how attractive, both physically and in her character, she was. Sarah would disclaim this straightaway – but it's true. She's physically beautiful because she's so natural-looking. She doesn't wear lots of make-up and she dresses casually, but then she has no need of falseness or flouncy attire to enhance her looks. Her complexion and athletic slimness radiate good health and fitness.

Tall, with short auburn hair, Sarah was then in her early thirties with a lovely long slim body. She had been born and brought up on a small farm in Kent which was taken over by the family in the 1930s. Her childhood was remembered as quite ideal. It was relaxed and easy-going but at the same time emphasis was put on education, especially for her, as it was assumed she would not come into the farm. After obtaining four A-levels she trained as an architect and after qualifying worked in third world countries and on urban projects. Although she enjoyed her work she never felt comfortable with it and had known for many years that her real joy was working in a farming situation. She was basically a very practical, down-to-earth lady who was never happier than when she was muddy and dirty and involved in tending live-stock or growing things. After working in Scotland for a while she went back to the farm to help the family over a difficult period.

One of her interests, she told me at the interview, was France. She loved the country and went there as often as she could. She then said that if she didn't meet someone special in the near future she would go there to live permanently – just work around different farms, maybe. At the moment she was learning French.

Sarah had never married. She was a friendly, outgoing person, got on well with people and was quite intuitive about others. She loved someone with a 'character'. However, she was very pessimistic about her chances and said to me, 'You'll never find someone for me – maybe you shouldn't even put me on your register.'

Out of the blue William became a member of the bureau. He had a strong character and a very pleasant and friendly manner. On our first meeting he seemed slightly shy, but not too shy, and five minutes into the interview he started to relax and be himself. In his thirties and tall, he was well built with broad shoulders, short brown hair and a great smile. He dressed casually and was certainly attractive in appearance.

William's home was in Oxfordshire; both parents came from farming families going back generations and had always farmed themselves. Throughout the years a large family farm was built up, and William's main wish as a boy was to go into farming as soon as he could. Therefore at sixteen he joined his father and worked exceedingly hard for a number of years. They expanded the farm, renting more land, and worked long and punishing hours – he was determined to succeed. But on reflection, he said, he had learnt the lesson that work, year in and year out, shouldn't be the most important aspect of life.

In his teens he joined the Young Farmers' Club, a nationwide network for rural young people, and attended for a number of years. He entered into all the social life and enjoyed it considerably. William had a small handful of girlfriends and just one important relationship. But after five years she realised she wanted to go back home to Australia and it would have been very difficult for William to follow her. They realised their relationship wasn't meant to last, and separated amicably.

William came across as being very hard-working. In his twenties he had worked his way around New Zealand and Australia for a while, doing various jobs on farms. On returning home he started to breed his own cattle and rented his own land. Over the next ten years he built up a reputation for producing really good stock, reflected in the prices obtained for them at the top end of the market. He had always enjoyed showing his pedigree beef cattle.

He went on to tell me at the interview that he very much would like to farm completely on his own account, and had decided that the best place to do that would be in France. He had been thinking about this for several years since farming had got far more difficult in Britain, especially without a farm of his own. He commented on how well young farmers are treated in France, and was adamant that this would be the best move for him.

He had been to the country twice to look at farms, and had sold his pedigree herd of cattle to another farmer who was restocking after foot and mouth. With the finance now available he wanted to take out a mortgage on a French farm and develop a good business. He was also taking a six-month course in French.

William admitted to desperately loving the land and the rural way of life, and all his interests were country-orientated. He loved 'open spaces' and enjoyed riding out with the local hunt. He took his nephew fishing, went rabbiting and really enjoyed going to game fairs and country shows. A sporty man, he played hockey for the Young Farmers and had for many years played rugby. His remote cottage close to the family farm lay about three-quarters of a mile down a track frequented by foxes, owls and all the wildlife you could wish for. The simple things in life meant a great deal to him. His love of wildlife was so great that, if at some time in the future he decided it was right to come out of farming, he could imagine working somewhere like a wildlife park. But of course he didn't really want that to happen because farming was his life and he felt it always would be.

Once I had got to know him well I could see the determination and the ability to get what he wanted. This 'grit', however, was softened by his easy-going temperament. He was a fair and straightforward man, treating people well, never losing friends and having high principles in all that he did.

William said he would like to meet a lady who would understand about farming. It would be nice if, when settled in France, he had a lady by his side. He could see a wife developing her own little business venture. However, it would be great if she understood the complexities and issues of farming so that he could share concerns and decisions with her. 'To have support in my farming life would be wonderful, and someone who was versatile and adaptable would be great,' he said.

As we concluded the interview he said, 'And I'd like to have children one day. Do you think you can work miracles and find this lady? I've only got four months before I go to France.'

'Wow! That's a tall order,' I said. But sometimes dreams do come true . . .

13
Come Live with Me and Be My Love . . .

Little did William know that I had Sarah in mind all the time. My second meeting with Sarah was three months after she had first met William. I said, 'Tell me, Sarah, you told me it was best not to put you on my register. Why was that?'

She replied, 'Because I thought the only type of person I knew I would be happy with didn't even exist.'

'When you got my first letter about William, what did you think?'

'Well,' Sarah said, 'before I started reading it I re-minded myself I'd already made up my mind to go to France, even if he was a nice man. Then, as I kept reading his profile, I thought how *very* nice he sounded. And then when I read that he wanted to farm in France I thought it was a complete wind-up – I seriously thought that some-one was playing a joke on me. I just never thought I would meet someone who wanted to do exactly the same as I did. My friends are wind-up merchants and they knew I wanted to farm in France, so I thought it was them putting the letter together. Then I realised they couldn't do that – they could not persuade you to do it, and it was definitely your headed paper. I remember sitting in your office when I said I wanted to farm and all that I told you about my perfect partner. I remember mentioning how I loved France.

'You'd said, "Blimey, that's a tall order!" But maybe you say it to others as well? So I knew I'd left you with a hard task. I even remember saying I'd like to meet someone who had a big smile. On William's profile you mention a big smile – great sense of humour and very down-to-earth. I truly thought it was a practical joke.

'I couldn't believe what he said to me the first time we met. He just sat there and said everything I'd been thinking for so long about farming. When we first met there were no worries at all. It was like meeting an old friend – no nerves, so relaxed. Never a moment when I thought, "Oh! My God, what am I going to say now?" We had so much to talk about – important stuff about big issues, not the usual polite conversation. We were straight in there talking about farming, on the exact same wavelength. We did it automatically. He was so easy-going – I'd felt so isolated because none of my friends seemed to understand how I felt about the farming situation. I knew they thought I was a bit daft. All the time I've been told by them it's too romantic and won't ever happen. "Get real!" they all said.

'I decided beforehand that I didn't want to imagine too much about William's appearance. I switched off, I suppose. It was because I didn't want to make prejudgements. That's why I didn't want any photos. A photo is just a still, and a person is full of expressions and so on. I remember once meeting a lumberjack type of person who thrilled me on the outside but turned out to be a weak-willed computer buff. It's great that William is tall and that he likes tall girls and was looking for someone a bit older than himself, as I'm just over a year older. When I read his profile I thought, "Pull the other one," This sort of person, the sort I have in my dreams, doesn't really exist.

'Immediately we met, I felt a spark between us. I knew it would be more than just friendship. I didn't let on, of course. We went to the zoo. I think I was a bit concerned about animals in cages – it didn't seem comfortable. Without me prodding him he said, "I'm not into zoos. I don't think it's right for the animals." We met at eleven, then had lunch at the zoo, and he left at about 4 p.m.

'When we parted – I still couldn't believe it. He said, "Do you want to meet again?" I wanted to say, "You've found your person to go to France with." But I actually said, "I think you should meet a few more girls as well as me, and if you don't find someone better come back to me."

'I could see he was looking worried and anxious when I said this. He said, "I don't think I want to meet anyone else. I want to meet you again." So we just left it at that. He tried to give me a little hug but I ducked away from him. I'm so shy. I know I give the wrong impression when I do things like that.

'He rang me up on the Saturday, two days after that first meeting, and I was really pleased to hear from him. We decided not to speak until the following Tuesday and it felt like years away. So I rang him up early as I thought I must show him a bit of heart, because I do hide my feelings. I said, "Tuesday seems such a long way away." He said he was very pleased to hear from me but was terribly tired. I thought, "Well, it seems he's not interested in me." He said, "I'll ring you tomorrow."

'When the next day came he phoned my mobile and asked if I had a landline phone near by. I was so pleased to hear from him. I gave him the number and ran over to the farm shop telephone. As I was waiting for him to ring back my heart started to go into my shoes – I really thought he would say he'd made a mistake. But he opened the conversation by saying, "It's seemed such a long time to wait to talk to you." ' She heaved a deafening sigh. ' "Thank goodness," I thought.'

I interrupted Sarah's narrative and commented on how incredible it was that they had met only once and just could not wait to be together again. She agreed.

'I really wanted him to come to my place,' Sarah continued. 'I wanted him to see the farm and the life I lead. The problem was I was extremely busy with the farm shop as it was virtually Christmas week, so he suggested he drove down to me. I was waiting for him outside the shop when he arrived. We had a good walk around the farm and he was really very interested and he chatted to all the others. I wanted him to meet my father, and as we were walking around we just bumped into my dad who was trying to repair a tractor. They had a chat about tractors and machinery in general and straightaway they got on really well. He called my dad a good old boy. I was pleased that he saw me, as me, working on a farm. It was good, because afterwards when I talked about the farm he understood all that I was going on about.

'We looked around the farm a bit more and I worked up until lunchtime. I had to pack up some produce for market the next day, and he helped me do that and move some stakes. We both prefer to be doing work. In the early evening we drove back to where I live – it's a very old farmhouse. I'd cooked a meal in a slow oven and so I was able to feed him quickly. I lit a fire, and as we chatted by the fireside he told me quite a lot more about his life.'

I asked Sarah what they mostly talked about. She said, 'Well, it was a real in-depth talk. William said, "We get on very well – we should make a go of it." As he said this I could tell he was slightly nervous. He was fidgeting, but there was a smile on his face. I was just smiling back at him, and I suppose I made him work hard at this little speech. He was pointing out how much we had in common and he thought we had a future together. Then he said, "Don't be too worried – I'm not asking you to marry me straightaway, you know!"

'I just laughed at him. Everything he said I agreed with, and I was nodding but not saying much. I'm much better at writing, and that day I'd written him a nice card which said I thought the world of him. And I thanked him for spending time with me. Then William said, "I feel so relaxed and happy with you. You make me feel so happy. . . . Do I get a kiss this time?" I was still a bit shy. So we had a little hug, but he had hurt his ribs so I said I must be careful with him and there was no kiss.

'Then Christmas came and I stayed with some friends a few counties away. Before I met William I thought I'd want to be alone. I really had got into such a despondent state in the previous months, but now I was eager to see all my friends. I could have spent Christmas with William, but as this was the first Christmas for his family without their mother, who had just died, I thought it right for him to spend it with his sister. We did ring each other up on Christmas Day.

'After Christmas, William wanted to cook a meal using a turkey he had in the freezer and he wanted all his family to come. He asked me to go along for this big family occasion. There was also a farmers' black tie event close to his home that he asked me to go to with him. Just before I went to his home for the first time I said, "Shall we do something a bit different?", so we decided to go to London, have a good walk around and go up on the London Eye. It was so different – it wasn't our scene, but it was interesting to see a different place and we had a lovely time. The previous day I had written him a letter which told him how I thought about him, and I gave it to him to at the little café at the bottom of the London Eye. "I'll get the coffees if you sit down and read it," I insisted. I explained that due to my shyness a man really has to chase me, and the sledgehammer approach would be more effective in getting the first loving kiss. A friend did ask me if we had kissed yet, and on hearing that we hadn't exclaimed, "Poor lad!" "Don't worry," I told her.

"I'll let him know when he has to take control in that area."

'The next time we met I went to his cottage. I was so apprehensive that he was going to give this big party at which I would meet his family for the first time. He cooked the turkey and I cooked the vegetables: it was instant teamwork. We were cooking for twelve and so we had to borrow some furniture. I was really nervous, but they were such good fun. I was so pleased to meet them all, and I could see how William fitted in. They were all genuine people.

'Then we went to the Farmers' Ball. He'd told all his friends about me, so everyone knew about us and how we had met. One of his brothers was great – he made me feel so welcome. I do love dancing and I was up there with all his mates and their partners. William told me I looked very smart and nice. He looked so handsome, and I was so proud to be with him. It was great dancing with him. All the farmers knew each other, and we had some great laughs.

'When the evening came to an end, we walked out together having had a fabulous time and I reflected that life was great. If you had asked me to write down on paper the type of man I thought I needed to meet I would have described William exactly.' Sarah didn't remember that she had actually done this in a letter to me.

She decided to delay the deadline she had set herself for going to France 'I was going off at the end of February and William had planned to go in about April. We changed our plans and arranged to go off the next week to spend a few days there. I speak a little French and William is learning.'

Now the routine is that Sarah works six days a week at the farm, then drives to William's cottage on Saturday night. They have decided that after their brief visit to France they'll come back for a few weeks and afterwards leave for good as soon as they can. Sarah said, 'I didn't want to set up in a place on my own – I've seen women get very hard being on their own. I just wanted to be part of a couple, farming together. The government supports farming in France, and they seem anxious to encourage the younger farmer to stay in the countryside.'

My conversation with Sarah finished with me asking, 'You came to me and said you wanted to meet a particular type of man. I think I've found him for you. Do you?'

She replied, 'He's just the person I would have made up in my wildest dreams. Even the "earthy instincts" that I knew in my heart I so much wanted to find are there. Yes,' she said. 'Thank you.'

When I spoke to William for the second time I asked him too about his first visit to the bureau office. I said, 'Tell me – you came to see about finding a prospective wife to go with you to France. When you left my office, did you go away hopeful?' He replied, 'Well, I really thought it would be months before I heard anything.'

I asked him what he had thought of Sarah's profile when I sent it. 'First of all, when I read it I thought she looked very bright. She's very brainy, you know, but it's odd that she doesn't like the academic side of life. I'm clever on the practical side, but where theory's concerned I'm just average. I was a bit naughty because I left Sarah's profile out at home and my brother read it by accident. He said, "Gosh! She's a brainy girl." 'But,' William added, 'she's an easy-going, down-to-earth type. We got on so well straightaway. Then she said I should meet other girls and if none of them was better than her I should come back. I didn't want that.'

I told him, 'When something good comes along that you've waited for so long, it's not always easy to recognise it – you don't immediately put your hand out and grab it, and I think that's what happened to Sarah.'

He continued, 'I was determined to get a yes out of her. We laugh about it now. Of course she did say, "Yes, I'll meet you again." I said to her, "I'll lay my cards on the table. I'd be happy to settle down with you." Then, when we went to the local Farmers' Ball, everyone wanted to meet her – she had a lot of teasing, but took it all well and she loved it. She got on so well with all my friends and looked so lovely, and when I told her that she blushed. Neither of us dresses up very often, so it was good to see each other like that.

'When we left the ball we'd had such a good time and she looked so beautiful that I decided to take command of the situation. I put my arms around her and told her that now was the right time for our first real kiss. That night I went and got a chain from my workshop and started fiddling about with it on my door. She asked me what I was doing. I told her I was just chaining up my bedroom door so she couldn't overpower me and have

her wicked way with me.' Sarah immediately collapsed
with laughter, realising how shy and sexually reserved
she had been with him throughout the previous weeks.
By saying all this William put her at ease and indicated
that they had all the time in the world to explore this part
of their relationship.

'So what are your plans now, William?' I asked.

'As you know, I've been planning for a long time to go
to France permanently. I don't think we should purchase
a farm immediately with the money I have. I'd rather
wait a year and work in the area, to get an idea of the lie
of the land. Of course Sarah was planning to go to France
to work, anywhere, on a farm. Her French is much better
than mine. I can order food and make a little conversation, but not as well as Sarah. She's bright and can help
with the necessary paperwork in getting set up.

'I know we'll come across problems, but I feel in our
hearts the two of us just want a good life together. I really
want to set up on my own, and I've said to Sarah I can't
be doing with arguments. The relationship I have with
her now is so different from any other relationship I've
had. I think about her all day now, and I find myself
smiling when I think of something special she's said or
done. Before, to tell you the truth, I could never understand why anyone wanted to get married. But now that I
know Sarah I can see why. She's a good genuine lady, a
rare breed. A real good country girl.'

I commented to William, 'When you go to France, it
will be a bit like pioneering when the early settlers went
to America.'

'Yes, but I was thinking just a few months ago that I might have to do it on my own. Now I have Sarah.'

As I travelled home my mind was full of excitement for them and for the new life they have found together. But do they realise what hard work they have in front of them? It will be totally exhausting, seven days a week, for a long time. But no matter how much I thought of the difficulties that lay ahead of them my spirits would not be dampened by hard reality, and I couldn't let go of the exhilaration and the pure romance of their life together.

14
It Takes All Sorts

March, April and May are the busiest months on a livestock farm. Most of the animals have been inside for the winter – maybe all of them if it has been particularly severe. Our dairy herd would have started to go inside at night in October, especially if the autumn was wet. By November they would be inside day and night. So by spring, for virtually half the year muck- and slurry-soaked straw would have been collecting and rising higher and higher in the sheds as each month passed.

The animals go out into the fields as soon as the grass has grown enough to sustain them. Usually non-milking animals are put out first, followed by the dairy herd when the spring grass has really come on well. The grass doesn't start to grow until the weather has got considerably warmer – usually late April for us, though the grass-growing season on farms at lower altitudes and further south starts much earlier. High up our limestone plateau in the Peak District, we are always counting the days until we can stop feeding silage and the cows can go out.

It's such a joy to wake up on these spring mornings and hear the birds singing and see the sun shining, just to feel some warmth and to know that the days of summer are just around the corner. I know people who live in towns feel this elation too, but with farmers the expectation of summer is often the only thing that keeps them going throughout those long winter months.

In March all the land is well worked to encourage the grass to grow quickly. We put fertiliser on all the fields first, then hope for some nice warm, wet weather which will help it take effect. This, combined with the muck from the cowsheds that has been spread over the land in the winter months, should do the trick. With a bit of luck, if we are able to start all the spring work in March everything might have been completed by the end of April. All the buildings and muck stores are cleaned out. The muck is dumped in a huge heap ready to be spread on the fields in the dark, cold days of next winter, when the fields are hard through frost and won't be marked by the heavy spreaders.

Next comes the harrowing. Every field is travelled over by the tractor pulling the harrows, which are like a double bed of metal spikes. This has the effect of ripping through the ground and breaking up any remaining large clods of muck deposited there the previous year, levelling any molehills and generally evening out ground that has been poached up or made uneven by livestock walking back and forth over the past year. Everywhere is then rolled with a cylindrical metal roller to flatten and make even the ground in the silage fields. This will help to depress any foreign objects or stones that, if left on the surface, could greatly damage expensive farm machinery.

As well as all this, the walls around the fields have to be mended. All the fields at Mere Farm are surrounded by dry stone walls built of limestone without cement. In the course of the winter gaps sometimes appear when frost dislodges the stones, and occasionally wildlife or cattle damage the structure. Dry stone walling is quite an art, and it takes years of experience to do well. John and all the men work on the walls, but our most skilled man is Harold. He has been our main waller for twenty years, and we get him to do a bit here and a bit there throughout the year. He's always been particularly good at circles and turns, which when you think about it must be very difficult to judge. It's a delight to see the results of his skill when he's built a perfect circle of stone around a mere. There's one mere close to the house around which he has built a ten-foot wall. It's truly a work of art, all completed by Harold Bonsall.

Gates have to be mended, and the baler twine which over the past year has invariably started to be used to hold some gates together will be replaced by proper hinges and fastenings. I'm always incredulous at the number of gates that farmers take ages to open and close because they are fastened with twine and other unusual attachments, or ones that don't hang properly and take the strength of two men to drag them across the field opening.

By the time all this spring work has been completed, the dairy herd will have been turned out for the first time since the winter. In the autumn, when it starts to get cold, dreary and wet, the doors of their buildings are left open for them to choose whether they want to shelter in their winter quarters or not. They really do choose the comfort of their sheds. Warm, away from the rain on nice dry straw beds with plenty of silage to eat, they can't be blamed. However, when spring arrives they are undoubtedly fed up with being confined and look out from those sheds at the sunshine and grass with longing. ('How do you know they have such emotions?' I'm asked. I know because I've seen the way they behave.)

I love watching those first few moments when they are let loose in April. At first they seem to freeze with incredulity. They stand and sniff the air, and then the reality that they are free sinks in. They start by running, jumping and dashing around with merriment and delight. Their tails go up in the air and they run all over the field visiting every corner, after which they start grazing very quickly as they can't believe they've got all this wonderful lush spring grass to eat. The men, John and I always stop and watch their enjoyment for the first ten minutes, but they quickly settle down and within half an hour are contentedly grazing and look as if they have never known winter housing.

At the same time we're lambing our sheep flock. John prepares well for the three weeks over which this takes place, setting up all the ante-natal and post-natal pens for the ewes well in advance. As a result our time in the lambing sheds can be used actually helping the newborns into the world and not constantly thinking about where they are all going to go.

Any sheep farmer will tell you that the worst aspect of

lambing is lack of sleep, because you have to be with them virtually twenty-four hours a day. Our basic routine to help deal with this problem is that John handles the lambing in the evening and throughout the night and one of the workmen is in the sheep sheds during the daytime. Ben and Sarah worked with the sheep when they were younger. It was the first thing they would do after getting back from school, and throughout the evening they would constantly be running over to the sheep shed and doing small lambing jobs. As they have got older, as for so many farmers' children, the novelty has worn off.

With all these jobs to do, there hardly seems to be time to breathe. Everywhere, however, does start to look as if it's had a good wash and brush-up. All the doors to the buildings are left open, and it's so satisfying to walk around and feel as if the whole farm has been spring cleaned from top to bottom – there's even a distinctive, earthy, non-mucky smell everywhere. Silaging doesn't take place for us until the end of the May, or even the beginning of June if it's cold and we've had bad weather. So, for a while, instead of the constant hustle and bustle, our everyday life assumes a more leisurely pace and we enjoy that lull between the end of spring work finishing and the beginning of silaging.

There is one job, however, that John dreads. I truly think he would prefer to go out and silage 100 acres than get that dreaded lawnmower out! He always has great difficulty with it after the winter, and I know to keep away from him at this time every spring. It never starts first time, so we have an inquest into what is wrong. Nothing that I can contribute in sympathy for the situation will be gratefully accepted. In fact, most Mays in the early years of our marriage we ended up in a great argument – all because of the lawnmower and its temperamental ways. Now, with experience, I just keep out of the way.

I wish we had had living close to us a young man who joined my bureau only a short time ago, when in his early thirties. At his interview he told me that, when he was eleven years old, he was so determined that one day he would have his own business that he started a lawnmowing enterprise. At the tender age of twelve he had forty-five customers including the local banks, had bought seven new lawnmowers and was employing six youths to work for him. He had sold the lawnmowers when he was sixteen and then started to develop a contracting enterprise. Now, only fourteen or fifteen years later, he had a million pounds' worth of machinery bought and paid for and a contracting business that employed many men throughout the year, working several thousands of acres throughout the southern counties. He had achieved all this in spite of being dyslexic and having to employ help to deal with his bookwork. He was an attractive-looking man who had worked very hard and now, at just over thirty, wanted to settle down. How I could have done with his lawnmowing skills over the years when, come what may, whatever you did or did not do, the blessed machine wouldn't start. Thanks for opening up the local tool hire.

So, on the annual occasion of the lawnmower coming out of the shed for the first time, I retreat to the bureau office. I sit quietly there by myself sometimes, and think about people's stories from the saddest to those that have the most wonderful endings. Of course, to achieve those happy endings people sometimes have to learn very hard lessons. And not all introductions are straightforward.

Some of the saddest situations in recent years have involved ladies of just over forty. I didn't come across this much twenty years ago, but now loads of ladies in this age bracket come to me and in all honesty it's very difficult to find introductions for them. Men of forty who haven't married are eager to meet only women in their thirties. It's still a bit of an old-fashioned world in that ladies of child-bearing age are in great demand, but as soon as they get towards the forties men look the other way. So men are still pursuing the dreams that men have had for centuries – to meet a younger woman and father children; but on the other hand there are women living the modern dream of the liberated sex wishing to be independent and prove their worth to one and all.

Nearly all these women have achieved a lot in their careers. They often have a degree, and right from university have believed that they had to succeed professionally. Marriage might have been in the back of their minds, but as something in the distant future. The years go by and, although they might have met good eligible bachelors, they have always thought there was plenty of time to find Mr Right and settle down. Getting towards forty, all of a sudden they hear their biological clock ticking – possibly for the very first time.

Some women have complained that everyone from their schoolteachers onwards encouraged them to put their career first and never warned them that they would possibly have to give up the prospects of motherhood in return. I sometimes despair at the naïvety of otherwise extremely intelligent women. Alas, I'm afraid many of these career women will spend the rest of their lives alone.

Only a short while ago I had lunch with such a lady. Anita had been on my register for quite a while. Her first introduction had seemed to go well, but after about a year the relationship broke down and subsequent introductions hadn't been at all successful. She echoed all the sentiments I've listed above. After working hard for many years she had attained her present highly-paid position. She had bought herself a large house and had started to work only a few days a week to give herself more leisure time. Over a meal in a country pub she confided in me that if she couldn't find a mate maybe she could have a baby before it was too late. She told me that the baby would need for nothing and that she would be able to spend more time at home than many other working mothers. She asked me, if I couldn't find her a husband, whether I could find a father for a child. 'Well, no, I don't do that,' I said. To which she replied as we left the pub: 'Please see what you can do.'

When given a challenge, it's very difficult for me to ignore it. I thought about all the pitfalls if I ever approached a man on such an enterprise. I must admit I did contemplate for a few moments whether I could work it, because at times I do hear from men who desperately want to have a child. I thought of artificial insemination, and then two doting parents, although living in their own homes and not sharing each other's lives, who would at least be able to share the life of their child. No, no – I couldn't get involved in this, especially since many men on my books who are anxious to have a baby actually want a son to hand their farm on to. Sons don't always come first time or at all, and if a son *was* born the father would want him to be brought up on the farm.

I decided to trawl the internet, and came up with several respectable clinics that help such ladies get pregnant through artificial insemination by donor. In fact those in the USA would send everything in a kit by post! Initially you decide which type of man you want to be the father of your child. You could print out the list – fair hair, dark hair, tall, academic, outdoor type, you name it they'd got it. You told them what you wanted and they reserved the semen for you. A kit would be sent to enable you to detect the few days when you would be fertile, and afterwards another kit would arrive by special delivery on your most fertile day – the semen specially ordered and packaged in frozen form for you to thaw out yourself and then inseminate yourself. I printed out all the pages and sent them to her, saying I felt I had done what she had requested and supplied her with a father for her baby. She's thinking about it very seriously. I was slightly surprised that Anita hadn't explored this avenue herself, but of course, as I've learned through my work, people don't always behave in predictable ways and using a go-between can enable people to take decisions they might be too nervous to take on their own.

There are some high-achieving women who go about finding a husband with the same efficiency that they apply to their jobs. Recently, a lady of forty-two wished to join who insisted that her introduction read both the *Telegraph* and *Spectator* (not one or the other but definitely both), played cricket, listened regularly to *Sorry, I Haven't a Clue*, and enjoyed poetry and classical music (not one or the other). There was no give or take – he had, without exception, to fulfil all those demands. I told her, quite bluntly I'm afraid, that I couldn't help. Similarly, the proprietor of a PR consultancy who had offices in central London wanted to join the bureau. Forty, with a PhD from Cambridge, she only wanted to meet a farmer who enjoyed scuba diving and played bridge and had obtained a degree similar to hers.

I feel absolutely awful when I suggest to a woman that her educational standards are so high that she would frighten off most men. I feel a traitor to my gender, who for decades have tried to claim equality in education. However, those are the facts. If a man thinks this way I don't believe he's worthy of the lady anyway, but there you go.

There has always been inequality of numbers in the different age groups. More young men seek a partner than young women, so men in their twenties and early thirties are at a disadvantage. Apparently there are always more boy babies born than girls, and this filters through to the marriageable age groups. The numbers start to be balanced on my register at about thirty-five and stay that way until forty, when more ladies come forward as long-term husbands go off with younger women. Men also tend to die younger from heart attacks, and this once again leaves the middle-aged woman alone.

I have my own radical ideas about this inequality in the age groups searching for a partner. I often think the best solution to the problem would be to turn all our expectations of a mate upside down and get everyone to look at life, sex and marriage from a completely different view. When an older lady finds herself alone, either through widowhood or divorce, would it not be such an advantage to both if she were to seek out a much younger man? If an alliance resulted, a woman of fifty would usually have her own home and financial means, which would considerably help a man of, say, twenty-five. He wouldn't have to struggle too hard to get established, he would possibly feel that children could wait until he was older, and what a fabulous boost to any lady of fifty to have at hand the attributes of a twenty-five-year-old male.

By the time the husband was about fifty one would assume that he would wish to have children and, as the older lady would now be in her seventies, she should welcome a new, second young wife to replace her. Any man of fifty would love to have a new wife of say twenty-five; he could provide well financially by that time and children born to this marriage would give the very much older first wife an interest in her declining years as a new 'grandmother'. The older wife would not be cast aside but would be respected as a mature and valuable part of the marriage.

I admit that this notion is a little simplistic. Men of twenty-five don't as a rule fancy fifty-year-old women, yet these days more and more women of fifty are still fit and look great. In theory, though, this would solve the difficulties both of so many unattached older ladies who spend years alone and of younger unattached men who also find it difficult to meet a marriage partner.

Other difficult introductions are those for men who are particularly short or particularly thin – maybe shortness is the worst. Most women like a tall man, and certainly one taller than themselves, so unfortunately when a man of five foot two applies to join I know his chances of success are drastically reduced. Sometimes if I can just persuade a lady to meet him that can be fine, because a great personality will often overcome shortness of stature. I've found that short men frequently have fascinating personalities: I suppose that, subconsciously, they have striven to develop something special to make them stand out. Sadly, however, no matter how hard I try, there always seem to be short men on my register who have never been able to meet someone special, mostly because women have just declined introductions to them and as a result they get fewer dates than other men.

There was one man whom I thought I would never be able to help, because of his physical disability. Harry, a forty-three-year-old farmer from Wiltshire, asked me to drive down to visit him. He said he didn't go out too much and wanted me to see him in his own environment. It was a small, livestock farm. When I met him I saw he was only about four feet four inches in height and had a severely disfigured back: a very big challenge for me. I suppose he had met that sort of reaction all his life, yet he still faced the world with a smile and great hope. I knew I couldn't be pessimistic with him and talked about his future with optimism and confidence, but we also talked about the reality of his situation.

We walked around his farm, which had been handed down to him from his parents. He was an only child, and really didn't have a lot of contact with other people except when selling his stock. His farm was immaculate. Not one blade of straw was out of place in the calf pens as I walked through his buildings. The alleyways were spotlessly clean and obviously washed down every day, and the calves looked in superb condition.

He had adapted all his machinery to accommodate his height and, although it was old, it was in pristine condition and sparkling clean. In fact everywhere looked as if it was endlessly washed – even the concrete throughout his yards was spotlessly white. Everything seemed so organised and had its designated place – wellingtons had their own little covered house outside the back door, and on the other side of the door were beautifully painted individual kennels for his sheepdogs. Since he didn't come into contact with many people, these dogs were Harry's sole companions for days at a time. The names on the kennels were lovingly decorated with painted flowers and birds. I had never seen anything quite so ornate for a dog, but it displayed his artistic talent to the full.

The house was a duplicate of the farm, beautifully decorated and tidy and clean. He showed me pictures of his parents, who had died a few years previously. Gradually, as I began to know him better, his character emerged and I began not to notice his disfigurement at all. Maybe this could happen to a lady, and maybe she could learn to love him. He started to relax in my company and said he wanted to show me something he had never let anyone else see. He set in front of me some handwritten poems that he had composed over the years, describing his loneliness and despair and his sadness at the way he looked. How painful to be as he was – the whole ironical and despairing tragedy of this normal man struggling to be recognised and treated as an ordinary person. I couldn't help but weep a few tears in recognition of how he had felt throughout his life.

I came away determined to do my uttermost for him. In the course of time many ladies did reject him, then one day a lady from Warwickshire joined who was only four foot ten inches. On her registration form she had written that her favourite pastime was writing poetry! I wondered if Gillian would accept an introduction to Harry.

I knew I had got to work very hard on this. Gradually I got Gillian to think about Harry in a very positive way. At first I got her used to considering about his lifestyle and character and their mutual interest in writing. Then I introduced the facts about his deformity, asking her to think hard and not immediately to dismiss the idea of meeting him. She got back in touch, and after much thought said she would go ahead. Because I wanted it to go well I accompanied Gillian to her first meeting with Harry, something which I had only done very occasionally. I was there when they first met, and sat between them talking to them both. Once I could see that the date was going well I discreetly left them together and retreated to a sitting room in the small hotel. A quiet place where they could walk in the grounds a little and sit privately, this hotel had been chosen with great care.

To my utter delight they got on very well together. Gillian said, as we were coming home, that there had been definite moments when she had forgotten his height and condition of his back and had begun to like him as himself and the personality he was. They spoke on the phone many times afterwards, and then Gillian went down for her first visit to his farm.

In no time at all I was told they were planning to get married, and soon afterwards a wedding photo arrived with a thank you letter. Then, within the year, I received another photo showing them with their new baby. I have to admit I was overcome with tears of pleasure at this wonderful ending.

There was not such a happy outcome for a very deaf lady who joined the bureau. For several years I tried to get introductions for her. I did so eventually, but all the men felt she was such hard work as they couldn't talk to her at all. I felt very sad when she came off my register with no success at all.

Tall ladies can prove a difficulty, but there is less reticence from men to meet them as they equate tallness with slimness, and visualise a modern-day version of Ursula Andress striding out of the sea with long, flowing blonde hair and a sexy, slim figure to die for. I have also very seriously been asked by one Gloucestershire farmer to look through my register and come up with a duplicate of Princess Diana.

Of course, the same barriers go up with overweight ladies, although not so badly as with short men. I would say about 60 per cent of men refuse to meet an overweight woman, but thankfully the remaining 40 per cent will. Facial hair on a woman is the biggest turn-off, and it's surprising how many women, considering all the aids on the market, don't use these to their advantage.

As I have said, men prefer, even in this equality-conscious twenty-first century, for a woman to look feminine. I receive comments from men along the lines of, 'She was wearing clothes no different from my own', and they often remark that they would like to have seen something that indicated there was a woman underneath. Women may say that it is, after all, their personality that a man is going to fall in love with. To a certain extent they are right. But the man has got to feel a sexual attraction, and that won't come about through an evaluation of her personality but because she seems feminine and desirable.

Other difficult introductions have been with people living in the isolated Falklands Islands in the South Atlantic, off the coast of Argentina and many thousands of miles from Britain. Their way of life, unchanged for generations, seems to be more British than ours, and the main plank of their economy is sheep farming. I suppose unmatched men in these islands naturally turn to the ads in the British farming press to help them meet a soulmate. When I first broach the subject of meeting a man in the Falklands to any lady, most simply cannot visualise meeting a man from such a long way away.

In the early years, when I wished to telephone a bureau member who lived on an outlying farm in the islands, I needed to know the times that their generator was switched on because without that power the telephone wouldn't work. I always used to communicate by phone, as it took so long for post to cross the oceans.

The first lady who agreed to an introduction was duly asked to go down there for a holiday after she had got to know the man by letter. I felt it was all very exciting and couldn't wait for her to tell me how she had found everything. She phoned me after about four days on the islands and described how, when she landed after an eighteen-hour flight, she felt everyone was watching her as if they knew why she'd arrived. By the time she'd been there three days the man she'd flown to see had asked her to marry him and she'd accepted. She told me she realised she could love him and the life on the islands, and so on the third day an impromptu engagement party was held at one of the settlements.

Her letter to me said, 'I returned to the UK for just three weeks to say goodbye to my family and tidy up loose ends, then flew back down to the Falklands. I wanted to get married here, as it will be my whole future life. After the wedding we moved out to the farm eleven miles away from our nearest neighbour.' They settled down and had children very quickly, but sadly a few years ago they parted and got divorced. She didn't return home as she loves it out there, and I understand from my latest bureau member who lives in the Falklands that she has married again.

It's hard to visualise the spread of land when a farmer says he has thirty thousand acres. My second Falkland Islander described himself as a quiet, good, caring man in his mid-thirties. Once again a proposal came very quickly after my lady client visited him, and I do know they are still very happy after ten years of marriage.

The next lady to fly down there telephoned me a few days into the visit and said, 'It's awful – I don't want to stay down here another day. I don't ever want to see another penguin as long as I live. There are no trees, and the scenery is completely dull.' So she promptly came home without success. However, a third marriage came soon after this and the couple in question are still happily married in the Falklands. My one disappointment is a father and son, both farmers, for whom I have been unable to find successful introductions. I totally understand the difficulties in finding local marriage partners. There are only about three thousand permanent residents of the islands, so it's like having to find a mate from the inhabitants of a large village.

Over the years men involved in farming from other parts of the world, mostly Canada, New Zealand and

Australia, have registered with the bureau. I also had a farmer from South Africa whose wife had died and left him with seven children. He was obviously anxious that someone special would come into his life rather quickly, as he had put ads in papers in Australia and New Zealand as well. I have to admit I couldn't find any lady who would consider taking on seven children in Africa, but he let me know that eventually he found 'his woman' in New Zealand.

As I was sitting in my office one day quietly going about my business, a huge shadow came across the door. I'd heard a vehicle arrive but I thought it was for the farm. Standing there was a near duplicate of Crocodile Dundee, dressed in shorts and a large sun hat and speaking with the deepest Aussie accent. He was on my register, and when I'd sent him a lady's profile to consider he'd decided to hop on a plane and come straight over and see her. No announcement: he just arrived as he was, still dressed for bush life. The lady I'd written to him about was an amazingly versatile woman, because when I phoned her that afternoon and said he had turned up she immediately said he should drive down to her and she would book him into a hotel close by. Thank goodness she took him off my hands. She went out to Australia for a while, but she didn't let me know if she came back or settled.

I was once asked to fly to St Lucia in the Caribbean for a week, flight and all expenses paid, to interview a lady who had a plantation on the island. She wanted to meet a Scotsman who would like to spend the winters in St Lucia with her and the summers in Scotland. 'You should really meet me,' she said. 'Come over and stay for a week.' I didn't, because I couldn't leave the children and the bureau just at that time, so unfortunately she never did become a client. Now, at this time in my life, if she asked me again I'd be there like a shot.

I've been asked what has been the most unusual type of man or date. The calculated approach comes to mind. A country bank manager who joined the bureau told me that in the course of the evening, when he was out with a date, he would at regular intervals go to the gents to do his calculations. He always took three pens with him – a black, a red and a green. There and then he would start marking down points for the lady he was with. The red would be for her bad points – danger, I assume; the green would be for her good points – green for go; and with the black he would add them all up. Only at the end of the evening would he decide if he wanted to see her again, depending on whether the green points outnumbered the red!

I'm also asked about the worst thing that has happened through an introduction, and I remember the very sad circumstances of one particular lady who had been introduced to a farmer. His photograph showed a broad, beefy, masculine man, and he was well educated. I introduced him to Elizabeth as they had the same cultural interests – music, theatre and concerts – and their ages were right and they were not far apart geographically. All had gone well and they planned to marry. Elizabeth had met his family and friends and felt very much part of his life.

When she telephoned again I thought it was to tell me about her wedding. It was, to a certain extent, but she sounded very distressed. 'We did get married,' she said. 'In fact it was a lovely wedding service and we had our reception at the hotel where we had the marriage ceremony. We'd decided to stay there for the first two days of our honeymoon. After that we were departing on a cruise from Southampton. But our wedding night wasn't how I imagined it to be.'

I held my breath – I had no idea what was coming.

'When all our guests had left and we eventually went to our room, I was utterly speechless when my new husband came out of the bathroom wearing a pink, flouncy, flowery woman's frock. I stood transfixed in shock. He then explained that he hoped I would understand his need to dress in this way, and even lifted up his skirt to show me his frilly ladies' silk underwear, which he explained he'd bought specifically for our wedding night!'

I was speechless on hearing all this – whatever does one say? Especially when she indicated that I should have known about his fetish. I did feel very sorry for her and started to utter the words that you would in such a situation. Apparently she'd walked out of the hotel that night and didn't talk to him at all afterwards. Her solicitor had set the process rolling for an annulment of the marriage. I regard this as the worst incident in the history of the bureau not because I'm criticising the man for his unusual preferences, but because he didn't have the decency or courage to tell his prospective wife and had gone into that marriage with deceit and dishonesty.

Not all my experiences are good, and as well as coming across dishonesty I've seen how badly unsupported girls can be treated. But even so, some of these stories have a happy ending. One day a delightful young woman in her twenties visited my office. An asset to any farm, Kitty was used to working with all animals. She was a relief milker, lambed sheep throughout the spring and was pretty and honest and sincere. Kitty came from a farming family, but both her parents had died and because the farm was rented it had to go back to the landlord and she rented a cottage. The first farmer I introduced her to courted her for about a year and then persuaded her, near to his lambing time, to give up her job and her cottage and move in with him and his parents. When their lambing was over and she had worked every day for the family without any wages, he told her she wasn't needed any more. She was devastated, of course, as she now had no home and no job. I asked her to come and stay with us as a guest at Mere Farm and told her she wouldn't be allowed to work – just to have a holiday for a while. I felt very responsible for the fact that she had lost everything in her life. Eventually, when her former employer heard of her plight, he offered her her old job back. But she still hadn't got her cottage back and had to take lodgings in her village. Sadly, despite the fact that most people who join the bureau are completely sincere, there will always be the odd charlatan.

The happy ending is that Kitty did come back on to the

register, although it took me some time to convince her that not all men are bad and to try again. She wasn't enthusiastic about her next introduction – just reluctant to have another go with anyone. He was a sheep farmer from Yorkshire, and before I let it go forward I spoke to him at length, to get to know him well. I was thinking about Kitty all the time when they were on their first date, because I desperately didn't want her to be hurt again. But this time they truly fell in love, and within a year they had a lovely country wedding in a little church on the north Yorkshire moors. They sent me masses of photographs of the wedding showing them walking out of the church under an arch of shepherds' crooks held up by local farmers. And now she's expecting their first baby.

A girl of twenty rang to ask if I could find her a husband. She said she had seen my advertising in the *Nursing Times* and wondered if I could help as she had to get out of the dreadful situation she was in. She hoped that if I could find her a husband she could get married immediately and leave her place of work. I said I was sorry, but I didn't arrange introductions just to help people leave their place of employment. My introductions were for love matches, not marriages of convenience.

I have always found that nurses enjoy connections with farming and the countryside, so for many years have advertised in nursing magazines. Maria explained that she had been brought over from the Caribbean to work for a couple in England: he was a solicitor and she was a nursing sister – hence the nursing magazine in the house, in which Maria had come across my ad. They treated her badly, paid her nothing, beat her when they wished, abused her, and she wasn't allowed to talk to anyone. In my naïvety I couldn't believe this kind of thing was happening in this country, but still said that regretfully I couldn't help.

As time went on she telephoned me again, just to chat and feel she had someone to talk to. Eventually she came to a point where she said she would kill herself rather than stay in her present life. I told John and he said, 'You'll have to do something about it.'

I knew I couldn't leave her like this. Next time she telephoned I asked her if she would like me to come and bring her to back my home. She was ecstatic, and I arranged to drive down the next day and whisk her away. I arrived on the doorstep when the solicitor and his wife were at work. I had never met her before, but, in gratitude and with only what she stood up in, she just left the house.

We drove home, and after a few days with us she started to relax and stop looking like a terrified child. We wrote a letter to the solicitor and his wife to say she was well and wanted to start a new life away from them, and I got a friend to post it from Scotland so they'd have no idea where she was. Maria settled into life at Mere Farm well. She began to love my children greatly, and after a while we got her a job looking after an old lady on the south coast.

It all went very well in that she saved hard and learnt to

drive and eventually bought herself a car. I would go and visit her about every six months and took great delight in letting Maria treat me to the occasional meal out and drive me about in her car. The old lady whom she looked after adored her and taught her how to look after a large period home. One evening, in the town she had made her home, she met Thomas, a tall, blond, handsome man whom she wanted me to meet soon afterwards.

She'd been going out with Thomas for about two years when the old lady died, leaving Maria all her beautiful antique furniture and quite a large legacy. This was the right time to move in with him. She set out her antique furniture beautifully in his home and was rapidly turning into a refined English lady. Maria then got a job in a residential old people's home for about three years. She learnt everything she could, and when they knew the time was right she decided to purchase a residential home for the elderly, with twelve bedrooms.

Maria runs the home, while Thomas has continued with his previous business. It's a classic large Georgian house with gardens all around, set perfectly on the south coast. Maria's antiques look striking in the private quarters. She employs a manager, cook, cleaners and about five other ladies, and supervises the whole enterprise herself brilliantly. I'm spellbound when I visit her and see how she has progressed. She drives me about in her BMW, taking me out for splendid lunches after she's spent a little time at her exclusive gym. I'm so proud of her when I consider how she's progressed from the day I whisked her away from her captors.

The lovely ending of this story is that she's now given birth to a gorgeous baby daughter. I was asked to spend a few days with Maria and Thomas just after she'd come out of hospital, for even this competent lady still seemed to want a mother figure by her side. During that time they asked me to be the baby's honorary grandmother, and hoped that she would always call me Nanna Pat.

15
Gather Ye Rosebuds

I started the bureau in 1982 and never imagined it would continue to exist for such a long time. I envisaged closing it down once I started to have a family, but its immediate success was so apparent that when the children did start to arrive I faced the fact that not only was I enjoying the work so much, but it seemed to be an essential service and the business was flourishing.

On the first anniversary I was amazed that I had been working in my chosen field for a whole year and that it was still going well. Each anniversary after that I would give a moment's thought to 'another year gone', but usually I was so busy on bureau work that I didn't deliberate too long.

When five years had gone by I thought it an incredible timespan to have been working at the bureau and felt I should mark it with some celebration. So on that anniversary in 1987 the *Farmers' Weekly* said they would like to do a piece, and asked if I could be interviewed along with some couples who had met through the bureau.

The day started with a journalist named Mary Wagner

arriving to interview me. I took her to my office and, as I do with clients who come for an interview, settled her into one of my comfortable armchairs with coffee at her side. There was no preliminary chatting about the day ahead. She was obviously a professional and keen to go straight into the interview. Her first question was certainly to the point: she asked me why a bureau of this kind was needed for the country community.

I wondered if she was a Yorkshirewoman, where I know they don't hang about with everyday social niceties, so I answered with precision and non-flippant replies. I described the geographical isolation that many farming and country people accept as their normal existence, their long and irregular work hours and, coupled with these two factors, the lack of confidence and shyness that so easily develop in these circumstances. Not always, of course, and no doubt organisations such as Young Farmers' clubs are invaluable in helping young people be more extrovert and confident.

I emphasised that a higher percentage of the rural population than of town dwellers have a quietness of character that is a definite hindrance when developing relationships with the opposite sex. And, given that they have fewer opportunities to mix with large numbers of the opposite sex, some rural people suffer great disadvantages when trying to meet a soulmate. I went on to describe ladies who have grown up in the countryside but find themselves in an urban situation through work, and find it hard to meet someone from the same environment that they were brought up in. You don't meet a farmer teaching in an inner city, and of course all this can add up to difficulties in finding that special person.

Mary and I then moved over to the farmhouse, and as each couple arrived they joined us in the sitting room. It is a long, narrow room with a conservatory at one end and a good view over the garden and fields. Immediately I could see that Mary was very interested in the assembled couples.

Giles and Angela sat on a settee together and described their wedding of a week previously. It had been a very quiet service in the little country church in Angela's village. They had then spent a week in the Lake District and had kindly returned a little early to be with us that day. They told the journalist that they were both in their fifties and had both been widowed quite early. Giles was a tall, slim man with receding hair and a weathered, thin face, but as straight as they come. He said he was a 'dog and stick' farmer. 'I first made sure Angela realised I wasn't landed gentry,' he joked.

Angela now worked as a farm secretary and did milk recording for local farmers. She was petite, with a lovely complexion, but very quiet in nature. She told Mary how she knew Giles was special on their very first date. Together they went on to talk about where they had been for their honeymoon and the life ahead of them. They had specific plans, which began with Giles retiring and selling his farm. That would allow them to move into Angela's cottage in a beautiful little village, which would give both of them a really comfortable life. Mary, I could see, was spellbound by this older couple who had found what so many others half their age had not.

Then Mary approached Eric and Gillian as they sat in two separate chairs drinking tea. I told her about their lovely wedding that I'd attended. They had been married for a year, and Eric described how he'd proposed to Gillian at her farmhouse as he was helping to dry the dishes. He was a gamekeeper and his wife had died about five years previously. Gillian was working the family farm; her husband had died several years earlier and, as well as a soulmate, she needed a man who knew about country life but hadn't got a farm of his own. 'That would have complicated things too much – we wouldn't have known which farm to give up,' Gillian said.

I recalled how difficult it can be to find a truly genuine man when you are a woman farming on your own. Over the years I have found that it isn't usually best to introduce a lady farmer to a male farmer. So often they are torn between farms, and I have seen relationships that could have worked otherwise completely fall apart due to neither being able to give up their farm. I continued to describe how men like gamekeepers and agricultural contractors are usually best for ladies like Gillian, as they are countrymen but don't bring the complications of owning farms.

We all had lunch, and afterwards Mary admitted that talking to my happy couples was enough to make the most cynical hack take a less jaundiced view of life. The *Farmers' Weekly* article appeared in the spring of 1987 and was called 'Mix 'n' Match'.

In 1992 the bureau was ten years old, and to celebrate that occasion I took a stand at the Royal Show. I had never done anything like this before at an agricultural show and was quite apprehensive. I really wanted to stand out and be different, but on the other hand I couldn't afford a large, expensive stand. So, for my small exhibit, I decided to veer away from the clean-cut lines favoured by people selling tractors or wine and have a romantic, hearts and flowers theme. The whole area was lined in a chintzy material printed with huge pink roses. Descriptions of the bureau's work were mounted on pale green material-backed boards which blended into the chintzy background. There was a patio area at the back where people could sit privately with me, and all in all I was very pleased with the romantically rural, garden effect.

I thought lots of new people would become interested in the bureau's work, take a brochure home and consider getting in touch a few weeks afterwards. This scenario worked to a certain extent, but in fact the stand mainly attracted many of the couples who had met through me in previous years. They brought their children to meet me, other members of the family were introduced, and the back patio hosted a continuous celebratory party for nearly a week. A great couple from East Anglia, who were one of my first weddings, brought their three children along to meet me. A newly engaged couple presented themselves, along with an accompanying grandmother. One couple told me about the birth of twins, which had not been anticipated at all. Living on a very isolated farm, she had not been to any ante-natal appointments. When she eventually gave birth they had the surprise of their lives when out popped not one but two large, healthy babies. But life doesn't always bring good news. Sadness came to the stand when I was told by one wife that her husband had developed an inoperable brain tumour.

I had some good fun on one of the days with the arrival of male twins from the Welsh borders, great big, well-built fellows who were so funny in their everyday speech. Everything was a joke and their lives seemed totally full of humour – but they wanted one thing: to find love and romance at the same time as each other. It was a good week at the Royal, but not a lot of people joined the bureau through my stand. Later, I learnt why. The big difficulty seemed to be that, as I was always there, people preferred not to come up and take a brochure. Apparently they felt I was going to pounce on them and embarrass them, maybe in front of their friends.

Now, when I occasionally put up a stand at a little local agricultural show, I go away, and by doing so I generate far more interest. I've been told from other stand-holders that the person picking up the brochure is often egged on in a jokey way by others, but really they do want a brochure and are secretly pleased they've got it and can it read quietly at home.

For the twentieth anniversary I decided to invite twenty couples who had been successful though the bureau to a celebratory lunch. They were people whom I had either never been able to meet personally but had got to know very well on the phone, or those whom I'd met previously but hadn't seen for quite a while. I decided I didn't want the press involved on this occasion. I wanted to take pleasure in the day with my special guests, and for them to enjoy themselves thoroughly as well. The arrangement was that they would all arrive at Mere Farm from about eleven o'clock. The farmhouse was spruced up, the bureau office redecorated, and turf had been laid to make a new small lawn. Fresh flowers were arranged everywhere, I had bought a lovely new silky ice-blue dress, and my present secretaries and several who had worked for me in the past were invited to meet everyone and join in.

Guests started arriving. Many, of courses had until now been just voices on the other end of the phone, and it was wonderful to meet them at last. The sun shone as John and I greeted everyone at the farmhouse front door. Some walked about the garden and a few, as we knew some farmers would, took it on themselves to walk around the farm and survey the stock – 'Can't they ever leave it alone?' one wife said.

Two couples arrived who hadn't yet married, and flashed engagement rings to everyone. One of them was from the southwest. He was a dairy farmer from the Bristol area and had told me how he usually milked three times a day, so he would never have found the time to go out and find a partner in life. But by joining the bureau he had met a lovely, sweet-natured young lady and they were planning their wedding soon.

As everyone arrived my secretaries (all the 'hosts' wore

a yellow rose to indicate who we were) served champagne on the lawn and in the farmhouse sitting room.
Then from about one o'clock everyone departed to the
local hotel I had chosen. It was a perfect place in that it
was only a ten-minute drive towards Dovedale and its
beautiful scenery. The hotel was extremely old, dating to
the sixteenth century, built of stone and with tiny leaded
mullion windows. It was also small enough to close its
doors that day to any other guests. Some of the couples
had booked a room for the night so they could enjoy the
day and evening without the worry of driving home
afterwards.

As we all assembled we were greeted with romantic
melodies from the hotel pianist, who had been drafted in
specially. Seventeen-year-old Ben and fifteen-year-old
Sarah handed around nibbles and carried trays of drinks.
The two of them complained at first about joining a party
of such old fogeys, but Sarah did actually enjoy the
dressing up. She was allowed to go out with a friend
and buy a new dress, and she chose the most clingy,
provocative pink affair you could imagine. Of course it
was foolish of me not to go with her, which I would have
done had I known what she was going to buy! She did,
however, look gorgeous. Ben had been bribed with cash
into wearing a suit. It was the only way!

The lunch was presented with interesting romantic
touches that the chef had taken great delight in designing.
Heart-shaped melon with ruby-red raspberries was the
starter. Swans made out of pastry filled with asparagus
tips – to represent, so the chef later told me, lifelong love

244

and devotion – accompanied heart-shaped smoked salmon for the main course. His inventiveness throughout was fascinating, and we were all intrigued to discover what would be presented next. Heart-shaped individual cheesecake was included among the puddings, and he had even commissioned a local chocolate manufacturer to produce special heart-shaped mints in a presentation box to mark the day.

After lunch we had some speeches for, unknown to me, my secretaries had asked a few couples to say some lovely words. John read out letters received from two successful couples in the Falklands Islands, wishing everyone a great day. I cut a celebratory cake and we all joined in a champagne toast to couples everywhere who are together because of the bureau. I sat back and looked on as everyone enjoyed themselves.

I looked at a couple in the far end of the room, laughing and joking with others, and remembered the man when he sat in my office and cried because of his stutter. I suggested he write letters to his introduction instead, but he was worried because he knew he didn't write too well. So I helped him write his letters. All went well, because the next time he visited me it was with his new wife several days into their honeymoon, and he still sat and cried at the joy and happiness he felt.

My mind returned to the happenings of that afternoon and I decided I should start to mingle with my guests. I was amused to see that Ben was quite convinced we didn't realise he was dodging out of the room regularly to have a cigarette, as he knew we wouldn't have approved.

He's growing up so fast. I was less amused when I saw Sarah making eyes at one of the younger waiters – whatever did she think she was doing!

The day ended in the early evening, with the couples promising to keep in touch with others they had met and myself. We all had such a good time. John and I and the children returned home in our taxi. The children went straight in but amazingly didn't turn on their loud music for once. I think they were both nicely mellow and about to drop, as they'd readily participated in the free drink. John and I sat down on our patio. You know how you feel when you've had such a busy day – you just have to unwind a little. 'I'm bloody knackered!' he said. I laughed, and without saying a word decided to savour the lovely day as I listened to the cows munching on their grass and enjoyed the scent of summer flowers that wafted through the air. After a while I became aware of another sound, quite hazy and repetitive – John was fast asleep and snoring. What a romantic end to the day!

The next morning I got up as usual and continued my normal routine of bureau work, reading through forms, matching up others and writing letters. I felt in some ways it was a new start; I'd completed the first twenty years and now I was beginning again and looking forward to the years to come. It felt good that my introduction agency had come of age.

With this milestone prominent that day I couldn't stop my mind soaring over thoughts that I'd hardly had time to touch upon the previous day. I thought of John, and remembered the pouring rain and the providence that had obviously decided to put us together, and felt very lucky that we had been able to enjoy such a happy marriage. It has often been said to me that a man can have everything – a large farm, good health and wealth – but all that means nothing if he wants someone to share his life with and there is no one.

Most of us have no idea how difficult it can be when you live in a very isolated country location or suffer from debilitating shyness and lack of confidence. But if only people could get out there and try meeting others – and keep trying. If you don't find a lover, you might find a friend – just keep trying, and don't think that because you're using an introduction agency you need hide the fact. So many people out there have found what they've been looking for – they didn't give up at the first hurdle, and success came their way.

Physical compatibility is of course important – I'm not in any way saying they must be beautiful, attractive or handsome, but for you there must be that little 'extra' that marks the other person out from the thousands of people you meet in everyday life. I sometimes ask people how they felt when they stood close to their introduction. Did they feel comfortable? Did the introduction smell nice – not a perfume or deodorant smell, but the right smell for you?

I do wonder if the new age of electronic communication is going to make a significant difference. It's certainly much easier to communicate at least on one level – that of talking and listening. But can you really have a satisfying relationship over the airwaves? If you're mucking out or in the milking parlour and your mobile phone rings, do you get a thrill of anticipation knowing that the girl you chatted to on the internet last night might be sending you a text message? How much better to hold her in your arms, look into her eyes and feel a responding hug.

As for what actually puts two people successfully together in a bureau setting I cannot really decide, even after twenty years of listening, advising, deliberating on problems, taking chances and learning from failures. Maybe all this adds up to experience, and what started to be an undefined instinct has come to be a refined skill. I'd like to feel, of course, that is so but I know that other elements come into the picture too. It could be coincidence or fate, or perhaps I'm just acting as a go-between for the powers that be. Maybe that power who knows everyone's destiny is just using me to put the whole jigsaw together.

I recently received a call from a lady in her eighties who explained that I introduced her to her husband when she was seventy-two. She described sixteen wonderfully happy years of married life. 'I'm letting you know that he died several days ago, at ninety-two, but I wanted to thank you for the lovely years I had with this great old man.'

As I put the phone down, her simple words convinced me that I had chosen the best job in the world.